MICHAEL PEDRETTI

Ciao Angeline,
Michael Pedretti

Diary

of

Giovanni Vener:

An Immigrant's Journey

to the

Heart of America

Book VII of a 12 part series titled

The Story of Our Stories

Pedretti, Michael 1942 –
story of our stories: /pedretti

Busting Boundaries, Williamsburg, VA

Print ISBN 978-1-09830-276-4

The Story of Our Stories is dedicated to the family whose lives inspired these stories. I would like to especially thank the mothers who time and time again planted seeds instead of discord; steering the sons away from war, violence and thievery.

I thank the following people who provided informative research to uncover the record of past generations: Dino Buzzetti, Alberto Cerletti, Inez Curti, Felice Ghelfi, Luigi Fanetti, Jean Pedretti-Flottmeyer, and James Venner.

I thank Susan Reindl-Thierman, Nicole Waite-Sudhoff, Leo Pedretti and Dennis Hamilton who provided valuable feedback and multiple corrections on early drafts of this work. I would like to especially thank my wife, Nancy B. Hill, and daughter, Victoria Pedretti, who graciously allowed me the time to write and provided moral support when I needed it.

Cover photograph by Christine Magnuson

Note: The *Diary of Giovanni Vener* is the seventh book in a series of twelve books that tell the epic story of you and me titled *The Story of Our Stories.*

Contents

I celebrate myself, and sing myself,

And what I assume you shall assume,
For every atom belonging to me as good belongs to you.

- Opening lines from "Song of Myself" by Walt Whitman

THE STORY OF OUR STORIES

Preface

It is possible that as many as 115 billion people were born before us. But you and I have each had more than one hundred billion ancestors since the first settlers arrived in the Valley of San Giacomo in Sondrio, Lombardy, Italy, around 840 AD. If you trace our ancestry back to the time of Caesar, each of us would have to identify more than 288 quadrillion grandparents or 288 million billion ancestors. If you would like to fill out your family chart dating back to the biblical Eve born around 4,004 BC, you would have to identify seven times as many people, or 1.6 to the 57th power. What if we go back to the year of Lucy?

You get the idea. There is no way, with that many ancestors, that you and I do not share a few billion of the same grandparents, making us not double cousins, not even cousins tens of thousands of times, but cousins more than a billion times over. Our genes are so intertwined that we are closer than brothers, closer than sisters, maybe even as close as twins. Yes, you and I, we are cousins—we are of the genes of Mitochondrial Eve, and we share the same genes of billions of her children.

The Story of Our Stories is our story. These tales are as much your tales as they are mine. "We have lived them together, we are living them together, we will live them together." We are not only twins, you and I; we are joined at the heart. To quote Walt Whitman, "Every atom belonging to me as good belongs to you."

According to Adam Rutherford, a genetics expert and author of *A Brief History of Everyone Who Ever Lived*, "All Europeans are descended from exactly the same people. Everyone (living in Europe) alive in the tenth century who left descendants is the ancestor of every living European (including Americans of European descent) today." A Brief History of Everyone Who Ever Lived, p 165

THE STORY OF OUR STORIES

Introduction

"I sing of arms and man"
—Virgil, *The Aeneid*

"I sing of kindness and woman"
—Pedretti, *The Story of Our Stories*

The mandate for an epic is to identify and celebrate who the people are and what their potential is. In Homer's and Virgil's eras, the epic hero was a male warrior whose violent behavior led to victories that inspired loyalty, patriotism, and submission to the ruling class. "I sing of arms and man," is the opening line of Virgil's poem about a brutal warrior who begets a bellicose Rome and the ancestors of the combatant Caesar Augustus. His epic celebrated empire builders, encouraged retaliation, and downplayed the massive cost of lives, enforced slavery, and legalized classism.

Should the modern epic celebrate dominance, war, and revenge? Will today's epic promote limitation, exclusion, and restriction? Is it not possible to put the historic, gentry-sponsored classism, war, violence, and tribalism into the past? Isn't today's hero the commoner, making things happen by mass commitment rather than individual supremacy—more interested in planting seeds than in accumulating power, in making advancements rather than blowing up people, tradition, and peace—more willing to fight for fair treatment with words than domination by war—more concerned with kindness than control—capable of letting empathy replace revenge? Today's epic hero is a planter: one who plants and cultivates; one who plans and nourishes. Our hero has no power or desire to raid the work of others. Our hero cannot come from the privileged class—by definition a people who rely on other's plantings to harvest their successes. Our story is not the story—cannot be the story—of someone indulging in the unjust wealth born of another's labor. No, our story is hidden in the mothers, "who long since left the shores of craving, supremacy and war to explore generosity, affection, and creativity." Come; join me in play, kindness, and song.

> I sing of kindness and of woman
> Serf no more, never Lord
> And of the suffering they endured
> Trodden under the might of the Sons of Misogyny
> Those ministers of misery who maltreated our
> mothers
> Turning brother against sister, husband against wife,
> Parent against child, mother against mother.
> Tell me, reader, how it all began, why so much spite?
> What did our mothers do to deserve their vengeance?

In *The Aeneid*, Virgil celebrated the Roman conqueror; I celebrate the planter of seeds. Virgil celebrated war; I celebrate harmony. Virgil celebrated dominance; I celebrate parity. Virgil praised father Augustus; I praise mother Eve.

The Story of Our Stories is the story of Marianna and Petronella, Peter and John, Adelaide and Stefano, and Agnes and her children. It is about the individuals who peopled the Mount of San Bernardo and who turned the roughness of Bad Ax into the gentleness of Genoa, but first and foremost it is our story, the story of you and me. Our story is written as an epic composed of twelve books, each with a supportive appendix. Each book covers a different story. Some cover the life of a typical family member of a specific generation; others reflect many people of a generation; another traces the entire story from beginning to now; and one looks into a future predicated by the behavior of our mothers. Each volume tells a critical part of the story, is an integral part of the whole, and plays into the unfolding of the epic. While part of a whole, each book can be read independent of the rest.

The Story of Our Stories

THE STORY OF OUR STORIES

BOOK VII

Diary
of
Giovanni Vener:

An Immigrant's Journey
to the
Heart of America

March 13, 1829 – March 13, 1900

[To the Reader: I have included in *Our Story* some
pages from the private diary of John Venner who immigrated
to Bad Ax, Wisconsin in 1856. He was born Giovanni Vener
in Campodolcino, Sondrio, Lombardy, Italy on the thirteenth
day of March in the year of one thousand, eight hundred and
twenty nine to Primo and Margherita [Della Morte] Vener.
He married Mary Madeline Starlochi, daughter of
Bartholomew and Mary [Zaboglio] Starlochi in 1867. They

had ten children and 38 grandchildren and at least 169 great-grandchildren. Even though Mary Madeline was 20 years his junior, she died ten months before John. John spent his 70th year on earth in the Vernon County Asylum for the Chronic Insane. In reading his diary, it seems he suffered from what we have come to call bipolar disorder. My dear reader, to save you the pain of his deepest agonies, the irreverence of his meanest thoughts and the fragmentation of his most muddled scribbles, I have not included John's most depressed or incongruous entries.

Almost indiscernible from age - scrawled in pencil inside the front cover - was a message signed by Lucy, one of the nurses at the Vernon County Asylum for the Chronic Insane:

"To Tom Venner: Some months ago I encouraged your father to write out his thoughts to help him cope with his illness. Usually we throw the notebooks away when someone dies. But these seem more than the scribbles of an insane man. I send it to you to do with what you feel appropriate. It seems you were his favorite."

Private Diary of an Immigrant

August 17, 1899

The priest came last night. I was hoping he brought the Extreme Unction. But no, he brought Douay-Rheims - I cursed him, told him to get out – "I don't need no Catholic God or any god for that matter" I screamed. "I want my Maddie, not your god damn God. If you brought some poison for my body I'd take it, but I ain't gonna read any of your poison for my soul." He was gone in such a hurry he left behind a book, a little book. I threw it at him, but he was running so fast he didn't hear me.

The nurse came over, picked up the book and handed it to me, "What the hell am I gonna do with a silly little priest book?" I screamed at her. "John, keep it till he gets back," she said in the damnedest, sweetest, littlest voice that made me want to rip that book into shreds. Instead I grabbed the chair, pulled it around just enough to scare her and then laughed, "I don't think he is coming back."

August 18, 1899

Primo bolted upright in the coffin, stared at me with those empty eyes accusing. I stood over him lying in a hospital - about to die. I leaned over the bed to kiss him on the cheek. I hesitated; he did not. His rattle startled me and then his breath stopped. Everyone was at the funeral. I touched his eyelids; his head too big, his mouth especially mean, he looked more a wax figure than a corpse. I kissed his forehead. He jerked up;

looked me in the eye. "Why do you kiss me now? Why not then? How could you let your own father die without a kiss? Now you kiss me?" he snorted with scorn followed by an interminable silence. "I'm dead," he bellowed. His laughter screamed across the room but no one looked.

I woke from my own scream. I bolted up in the bed and stared into the darkness; the streetlight barely shining through the window creating deep long shadows. "Dad, Dad, Primo," I screamed. I scared myself. I opened my eyes, arms up to protect myself, searched the corners in the dark of night, "Where are you?" I yelped at the top of my lungs. "Dad, where are yoooouuuu?" But he does not answer; he is not here.

Sally - she's the pretty nurse - opened the door, "John, you alright? Nightmare again?" I lied, "I'm fine Sally, I just need a warm woman by my side, want to come to bed?" She left.

I wasn't there – at Primo's death or his funeral. He died in our old house back home, I am here in America, in Bad Ax - no, I don't think this is Bad Ax anymore. We changed the name to Genoa. I am just up the valley, in my house, with Maddie. No, this is not my house; this is not Genoa, "Where is Maddie? She's dead isn't she? I know she is dead. Where am I?"

It's morning now. In the middle of the night, when I realized Maddie was not here, was not there, was not coming, I went to the door. It was locked. I pounded and kicked and shouted through the little window with bars, "Where am I? Maddie, where are you? Where am I?" Sally came back with her two big militia men. They tied me to the bed and put their muzzle on me. Do they think I'm a mad dog? I don't know if I got back to sleep. But when I woke up, the muzzle was gone and my arms and legs had been freed, but I was in a strange dark room with several other beds and not a person to be seen.

I know where I am. In a little prison where Ursula locked me up. Some daughter she turned out to be – traitor. I want out of here. Where's Rocco? He could get me out. Where is my son?

August 19, 1899
Dear Maddie,

The people here think I am crazy. One of them gave me this note book and said, "John, this is for you to put down your thoughts and feelings. Some of our patients have found it very helpful to write how they feel. Some who wrote the most even got to go home." I wrote a couple of entries, and it was nice to write again. I don't remember taking the time to write down my thoughts or ideas since I left Campodolcino [Ed. Note: This is town where John grew up]. But still it felt empty – why was I writing? After I had that dream about Primo, they locked me in a dark room. It was horrible, but while there I remembered how I had dreamed of writing when I was young, how I had even begun to write a novel based on Grandma, and I decided if I got back to my room, to some light, I would write you a letter so I can tell you what I am thinking, what is happening. Maybe, just maybe, wherever you are they will let you peer over my shoulder to read my letter of love to you.

It is very nice to have some light after being in the dark so long. I'm going to leave you now and look out the window.

Oh Maddie, it's almost corn harvest time. There is the

biggest field of corn I ever seen just outside my window. Looking over the corn turning brown with gilded tassels, I saw you driving Nellie out to the field to pick up a wagon full of corn. The sun behind you made your hair look like fire on Nellie's shoulders. And what shoulders that horse had. She walked forward with more pride than a horse ought to have and you walked behind with so much dignity I got aroused.

Where is Nellie? Now that is a horse. They used to say around Genoa that ole John Venner and Nellie could plow at least an acre more than any other farmer. I'm not so sure that was true, but in our day, we sure could out-plow anyone in sight. What a horse my Nellie was.

I can still out-plow any of those young whipper-snappers who like to flex their muscles around the young girls. All show and no doggedness. Nellie and I could still plow one and one-half acre of clay today. There ain't another man in Genoa who can plow a full acre between cow-milkings.

INSANE ASYLUM, VIROQUA, WIS.

Vernon County Asylum.

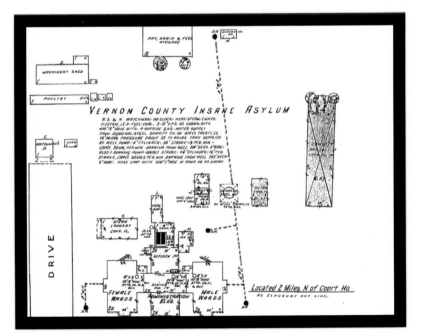

Mary Madeline Starlochi Venner.
1851-1899

Nellie

A cold day in September

I think it is now September.

September 18, 1899

Momma used to say, "Always ask yourself before acting, 'Is the reward worth the cost; is the cost worth the reward?'" Momma, life was not worth the cost. The cost was by far too high. You never gave me the chance to ask.

September 19, 1899

Dearest Maddie,

Maddie, I miss you so much. Just now, I was staring at the overgrown cornfield and I thought how you and I and Nellie would never have let it go to the devil like that. But the thought of you made me long to be with you to talk with you. I know I can't do that, but I have this paper and this pencil and I can write to you, so from now on I will write you a letter every day.

I am in a nuthouse. Can you believe it? Giovanni Venner, Mr. Thinker, Mr. Strong Man, Mr. Giv'em hell Johnny, Mr. I Can Do It - locked up in a loony bin like a helpless puppy having his dinner presented, taken for a walk every day, told what to do, talked to as if he did not understand. I understand just fine. I understand they are the ones that are nuts. Every one of them is as crazy as a peach orchard boar.

Maddie, come get me. Save me from this insane place. Come play with me. You are why I woke up in the morning, why I could look in a mirror without disgust, my angel, my goddess, my breath, my field friend, my concerned confidant.

Grandma, the wisest person I ever knew, told me we all needed to have three loves in our life. She called the first love one of infatuation – love at first sight. A joyous love but one filled with pain and angst. The feeling of having heart strings woven into one when your love is in sight and the feeling of being ripped apart in separation. Dominated by possession and jealously, the ability to move inside this restraint is not possible. Our second great love is one of lust – intense physical intercourse that seems to obliterate all else. Grandma said if we were lucky enough not to marry the object of one of those loves, we stood a chance to find happiness in marriage where communion, creation and playfulness were possible. Grandma encouraged me to have and terminate the first two so that the third would become possible. When challenged, she did admit it may be possible that the three stages could be had with the same person and that happiness was possible if the couple waited until they reached the third level before consummating their relationship. But she added, "Yes it is possible, and it is also possible you will become Pope." Oh Grandma, I never became Pope, but I did become the Pope of Lovers, finding all three stages of love in one woman and she in me.

Maddie, for the longest time I thought I would become Mr. Bachelor, the man with it all who in the end had nothing for he would grow old in his victory as lone man without love, without care, dying alone in dirty clothes, rotting on the floor of his little mansion found many days maybe weeks after I died of emptiness. I looked and looked for the woman that would spin my heart into passion. Not to be had. A woman that would make me lust seemed not possible. I first saw you, as a woman that is, with tears in your eyes as you observed death in your Grandmother. Your beauty shone in your compassion, your loss, your strength, your spirit joining as one with your grand-mom. You were so young, yet so old. I was smitten, and I understood for the first time what my grandma called infatuation. And so I watched you from a safe distance, enthralled on one hand but feeling like a dirty old man on the other. As your grip over me released, time again became possible.

I see it now like it was this morning. The virgin, in blue, the sun behind you, the sun in my face, our eyes meeting along the creek where you had come to gather walnuts and I to find Belina who had strayed from the herd. I had put you out of my mind, had known from the beginning that you were too young, I too old. Later, you told me that you had developed a schoolgirl crush on me but had giggled to yourself how Mr. Old and Miss Young would make Mr. & Mrs. Odd. Before that moment standing in the dew of the morning, we had carried our secrets then buried our feelings deep in our hearts. I don't know what you saw, but I saw Mona Lisa glowing with freshness, alive, wanting, looking into my eyes as if I were. The stillness was celestial. I said, "I better find Belina. She's been gone from the herd for too long." and moved to leave. You replied, "John, you never know what might happen." No moment stands so vivid in my mind.

The next morning when you came to collect the day's harvest of walnuts, I was waiting. We both knew what we wanted, but we also knew we had to wait.

And so we did. As you approached your 17th birthday, you told me your dad was arranging a marriage between you and George Beffa. I spoke with your father, whom I had known as a boy when we both grew up in Campodolcino, but he told me he was determined to marry you off to the Beffa boy and that I was too old for his Madeline. You swore you would not marry anyone but me.

"Then we must marry."

"I am ready" you said with the tenacity of a woman who had come of age. Your determination was taxed when your dad did everything he could to stop our marriage, but in the end he walked you to the altar and we wed; two virgins never more crazed to deflower each other. Our lust erupted as the crops waited, the cows barely got milked, and the weeds flourished.

Yet it is not that time I remember so much as our moments together, walking to the field hand in hand, laughing at dinner, planting and harvesting as a team, tending a sick cow, butchering a chicken, finding some time each day to play together and with our children before the evenings descended into darkness. I recall ever so vividly the day when Father Wirtz preached you had to work at marriage and after the service you said, "No Father, by the time you have to work at marriage it is too late, you have to play at marriage." And it was that playfulness with which we did everything that made life with you so perfect. Even in planting and harvesting season when there were never enough hours in the day to complete the tasks at hand and you worked side by side with me to complete as much as possible, we never "worked" at it.

Come, Maddie, play with me. It is in the playing that we found life, ourselves and each other. Come now, play with me.

September 22, 1899

"I haven't seen you before," I said to the stranger in the mess hall. I noticed that the wrinkled old man I was looking at moved when I did. I stuck out my tongue at him. He returned the favor. I moved left, he moved right. I lifted my finger he was right with me. Then I realized he was me. "When did I get that old? My god." I did not recognize myself. I looked so old. I mean really timeworn.

I went for a walk. Had to prove to myself I could still walk; that I was not that dilapidated old man I had seen in the mirror. The walk did not help. What would help is if they would let me die. There is no reason to live to tomorrow. What's here – four walls, a bunch of mean crazies, stench, cold, it is a hell hole. I am going to rot. There is only one thing to look forward to. That is to join you, Maddie. Why don't you come and take me? Maybe you ain't there either. Maybe there is no there. I don't think there is. I don't mind – nothingness would be so much better than this. I want to be with you, but if there is no there, I can't miss you, can I? Here, longing for you, being treated like a dirt child, it is only knowing that soon it will end that keeps me going. Ironic is it not? Maddie, whisk me away. Please.

October 2

Dear Maddie,

Father Mono came back for his little book. Guess it took him a couple of months to get up the courage. He looked so pathetic, I was nice to him. Told him I was having a bad day when he came by. Told me his congregation included Rising Sun and all of Viroqua which included the nut house [to be fair, he did not call it a nut house]. Then he starts up on the Jesus stuff and how I need to read the bible and he has one in his office and he will go get it for me. I tell him to shove it. He handed me back the little book, "John, I'm going to leave this here. Read it if you want." Read it if you want? What was he thinking, who has time to read, there are fields to plow, seeds to plant, hay to make, horses to feed, cows to milk, don't have time to read the newspaper let alone some stupid book.

"Giovanni," I said to myself - sometimes I call myself Giovanni. "Giovanni," I said, "you got no hay to make, there are no horses here to feed, no cows to milk, there is just you and four walls and a door they keep locked with bars on the window. You got plenty a time to read." I thought, John, you haven't read a book since you left Prestone. I recalled reading Alessandro Manzoni's *I Promessi Sposi* for school. Pretty damn good book. Dante? Oh my Dante. I hadn't thought about Dante since, geez I don't remember. I had not read one word of Dante since the ship. Not since the ship, when that crazy German bastard threw my *Commedia* overboard. Just grabbed my copy from me and tossed it overboard like he thought it was the devil. Must have thought books were the work of the devil. Now there was a guy who needed to be locked up in an asylum for the chronic insane.

Why didn't ole Mono bring me Dante? Yea I could read some Dante. Especially the inferno part; I been to hell but not back. I wish I had the *Inferno* here. I do.

October 4, 1899

It's tomorrow. I forgot what it's like to read. This book Fr. Bona or Mono or Rono or whatever his name is gave me –

it's a little book called "Leaves of Grass", by a poet I never heard of who calls himself "Walt Whitman, an American, one of the roughs, a kosmos, Disorderly, fleshy, and sensual.... eating, drinking and breeding..." I read it cover to cover, read the poems again, I couldn't put it down, read the first poem again until it was so dark I couldn't see the words. Maddie, you'd have loved this, book. He describes you to a tee: He calls you one of "the numberless unknown heroes equal to the greatest heroes known." And he captured how I felt so many mornings: "The song of me rising from bed and meeting the sun."

I wonder if old Rona Mono read these lines:

Divine am I inside and out, and I make holy whatever I touch or am touched from;
The scent of these arm-pits is aroma finer than prayer,
This head is more than churches or bibles or creeds.

A funny thing for a priest to give to a skeptic like me. I don't suppose I am really an atheist. When you were laying there, your beautiful body slipping away, I made an oath. Spare my Maddie and I will never doubt you again, I will even go to church with Maddie; take her and I will know forever there is no god. I know you wanted me to believe, but how could I believe in a god who was used as a tool for the rich and the priests to subjugate the rest of us? If there was a god, he would not let that happen and he would not have let my Maddie die before me. I don't think god is dead, how could he be dead if he never was?

October 5, 1899

Dear Maddie,

Mr. Walt Whitman wrote, "What is man anyhow? What am I? And what are you?" I ask one last time, "What are we here for?" I remember you used to get mad at me when I would start a conversation with this question. Now I have to think about it again. No way can I buy into the idea I was born so I could suffer and earn my way to some glorious afterlife. My god, my friends, what are you thinking? That idea needed to be put to rest along with the idea that the earth was the center of the universe and the sky revolved around us.

Maddie, I ask the question one more time. What is life? Remember the word game we played with the children where we competed to reduce an idea to its referent, the element without which the abstraction could not exist? If that was not possible, which word still in the game was the most essential? The one I remember most vividly was book. I said "cover" and Ursula picked up one of her old classroom books with the cover long gone and asked, "Is this still a book?" We eliminated illustrations, page numbers, index, editor, and many more, but in the end we all agreed; to have a book you had to have printed words, paper or the equivalent, and binding.

We should have played that game with the word "Life." I tried it myself this morning, and the first thing that came to mind was Paul. No I didn't mean Paul is a concrete word for life. That sounds funny. I never been much into the Christian thing, and I certainly think Paul had some odd ideas that ought to be ignored by all. I recalled that he had some ideas about life and love in one of his letters, so I asked Lucy for a copy of the bible. Sure enough, he was onto something in the *First Epistle to the Corinthians* when he asked [and answered] the question, what is the one thing you cannot be without, live without, and still consider yourself a human. What does it boil down to? I think Paul was playing an early version of this game. He asked what makes a human - what gives meaning to life? Paul gives the answer away immediately. "Charity." It is the referent – the state of being without which the idea of life is not possible. Without charity, Paul claims nothing else matters; the essence of humanity is charity. As the letter progresses he says prophecy will fail, tongues will become silent, knowledge is ephemeral; the strongest faith in the world can still leave me as "nothing." Even giving to the poor, if not given with charity, will be of no value. We can give from fear, out of guilt, in hope of increased returns, motivated by pity; if we do, it is for naught. Unless we give from charity – from love, it is to no avail. Paul concludes there are three key words to describe life; faith, hope and charity. Paul states we can live without faith, even without hope, but without charity, there is no human life. The absolutely essential referent for human life is charity.

That leaves us with the question what does Paul mean by charity? Certainly he is not using the term in the modern sense of giving to the poor. Paul goes on to tell us what charity is not:

> Charity envieth not; charity vaunteth not itself, is not puffed up
> doth not behave itself unseemly, seeketh not her own, is not easily provoked, thinketh no evil;

Rejoiceth not in iniquity.

So what does he mean? I believe he means being outside of yourself. Being connected to your family; that is to your wife, children, parents, relatives, friends, to all mankind, to all living beings, to the universe. Paul says if we are ruled by envy, pride, arrogance, greed, anger, revenge, and injustice, we cannot know life. Any of these vices prevents a meaningful life. It reminds me of *Inferno*. I'm trying to remember Alighieri's divisions of hell. It's been too long.

Paul defines charity as:
Charity suffereth long and is kind
Rejoiceth in the truth

To restate Mr. Paul again, the three things needed for charity are to be kind, seek the truth and endure. I don't get what "suffereth long" means. If it means we have to suffer to know charity, I think Paul got it wrong on this point. I know there are plenty of pagans and Christians that think you have to suffer, - wasn't that a Sophoclean principle? I cannot agree. Life ought to be enjoyed. Man was made to play. I worked my ass off my whole life, but that does not make it correct. You and I suffered through the great recession of 1893. That was not necessary – we were the bird turds of the greedy rich – without their voracity we would not have suffered. Sure, sometimes nature wreaks havoc with our lives, but we can weather that. Some think we weather it better if we had suffered in preparation. Baloney, suffering weakens our resolve, it does not provide more resilience.

October 6, 1899

Maddie,

You won't believe who came to see me last night. Dante Alighieri, as big as life, stood over my bed and smiled. I did not recognize him at first. He did not look mean or like a Roman master. He did not stand 6 feet tall, had no scowl on his face, but was a short, rather balding, a little on the pudgy side charmer who had a gleam in his eye, a broad smile, and a break-your-eardrums laugh. He looked me in the eye, took on a huge grin that turned into a raucous laugh, "You know who I am?" I shook my head. "Oh yes you do," he twitted. He looked a little like a northern Italian. "Uncle Giovanni?" I asked on a lark since I had not seen my uncle in over 40 years. My guest rolled over to the floor in laughter. I was not about to take another guess when he said, "I am your favorite poet, Alighieri, Dante Alighieri." Was he here to take me to heaven? I said, "I'm ready, heaven, hell or purgatory, I am ready." I thought Dante would not stop laughing. But he did and he said, "You are very funny Mr. Vener." And he laughed some more. I said my name is Venner, not Vener anymore. I am American and in America everyone says Venner, so I am VENNER." He looked at me scornfully with an "are you kidding?" roll of the eyes.

"No John, I am not here to talk about the afterlife. Not to worry. No, what you need to concern yourself with is this life – the one you are living now – right here in this asylum at 2:18 AM on the sixth day of October in the last year of this century. No more whining and feeling sorry for yourself. No more efforts to die. No more wishing you had written that book about your grandma, no more penny philosophizing, no more writing letters to Madeline, my god, Johnny, she is already dead. What is it you are thinking? Johnny, you have in you the story that must be told. Whitman has nothing on you. *Comedy* is a mere prologue to what you can and must write. For you have known love, you are the quintessence of kindness, you are the planter, the creator, the one who seeks, the domestic intermediary who sees the interrelated connectedness of the trinity even as the power is in the circle.

I got it wrong John. Hell is not hell because its inhabitants lack hope, but because they lack kindness, creativity and empathy. It is you - through your momma and her momma and her momma and papa - who knows, who must tell the story. You have what it takes to write the epic about the common family acting with kindness."

October 8, 1899
    A little song I sang today:

The lunatic
The lunatic is carried
The lunatic is carried at last
The lunatic is carried at last to the asylum.

The lunatic is carried at last to the asylum a confirmed
    case.
He will never sleep any more as he did in the cot in his
    mother's bedroom;
The lunatic is carried at last to the asylum a confirmed
    case.

He will never sleep any more as he did in the cot in his mother's bedroom.

In his mother's bedroom
The cot in his mother's bedroom
He did in the cot in his mother's bedroom
Sleep any more as he did in the cot in his mother's bedroom.

Whitman speaks to me again.

Saturday, October 14, 1899

[Editor's note] Dear reader, John had a very bad day. Some of his entry is illegible and what can be deciphered is too dark, too desperately depressed and much too violently graphic for your eyes and thoughts.

Sunday, October 15, 1899

"This hour I tell things in confidence,
I might not tell everybody but I will tell you." -ww

Been reading all day. Reading the only book I have here - over and over - Whitman's little book of truths. That's how I think of his book, not *The Leaves of Grass*, but Whitman's *Little Book of Truths*. I should write a little book of truths – write a few doggerels highlighting the main things I have learned. It might include:

Every child should inherit something – we all made America what it is but some got rewarded more than others – shouldn't everyone's child reap some of the benefit? Why should the slave owner's child inherit wealth beyond his remotest need and the slave's child inherit debt?

The American myth is that capital makes jobs. Quite the opposite, labor makes capital. Capital does not grow on trees. It is the fruit of labor. Just because some capitalist over the last half a century skimmed off the top and concentrated large amounts of capital in their pigsty does not mean that capital grows on trees or is concocted out of the dung of pigs. No it grows on the back of the laborers the swine like to malign with their propaganda.

Education is great in America because it is local, serving the need of the people. The state and federal governments should stay out except to help equalize each American's opportunities by providing no-strings-attached grants to the communities of the poorest 25% of the population. The children born in the poorest areas did not choose that and do not deserve to be punished with an under-funded school.

The federal government should establish an account for every child born in America that can grow until retirement. We should not be putting our elders out to pasture or in asylums for the mentally insane.

I have more certainties, but I am too dog-tired to write them down now.

October 18, 1899

The inside of me is possessed with mold and rot, my mind is molded jelly, and my being longs for discharge. Life is too painful. Come, Death, come. When I was young I thought immortality was the right thing for Giovanni Vener.

God forbid. To live in this inferno for eternity, with a body that screams from within – now that would be hell. I must go, makes no difference where - to void or to Maddie and her God. The point is to get away from this disillusioned, disintegrating, dissatisfied, dysfunctional, disserviceable, decomposing, defunct body and mind. Death, hear me, I await your company. Do not be late, for our time to rendezvous is now.

October 19, 1899

"Great is today, and beautiful,
It is good to live in this age....there never was any better." –WW

October 20, 1899

The sixth president got it right. The goal of the government is to improve the economic, intellectual, and cultural life of the country. Too bad he was blocked by the warmongers and the entitled who had unlimited resources to convince the public in the errors of their ways. No president since has dared to dream. I think this should be the last truth in my little book. Note to myself: I must articulate the discernment of Adams' wisdom in such vivid language the entitled and their warrior supporters' propaganda cannot dull the public's astuteness.

October 21

Here is an idea for one more chapter of "Venner's Little Book of Truths"

I believe every man can reach his potential if he follows these seven steps:

- o   To be glad to be here and now
- o   To be glad others are here
- o   To have something to say
- o   To appreciate that others care about what you have to say
- o   To be centered physically, mentally and spiritually
- o   To be outside of yourself
- o   To act with courage and a social conscience

October 23, 1899

Dearest Maddie,

I had that dream again. You know, the one with Primo sitting up in his coffin. But this time I woke up before he could yell and laugh at me. I started having that dream after you died. Why did you die before me? Without you, breath is not possible. Sometimes I just want to tie the nurse in the room and run all the way to hell.

Some days I can hardly get two thoughts together, I just want to die; there is nothing to live for. But today I am ready to get out the horses, plow Tom's field, bring home the cows to milk like we did in the old days. I ache to pleasure you into conception.   I yell at the nurse to let me out, I need to run home; she tells me I am in Viroqua, "At your age no way you can make it to Genoa on foot. I bet you could have when you were a young Atlas."

Maddie, I am Atlas. I hold up the world. McKinley, move aside, I will be President.

Later today:

Maddie, it is later. I am exhausted, I think, from holding up the world. Now that is an asinine idea – I do not know where it came from but I see I wrote it earlier today. I don't know what happens but sometimes I know I can do anything; then suddenly and without cause I am reduced to muck. Sometimes, things almost seem normal, like the old days. But it does not last. I want to tell you how it feels, what it is like. But I can't, my Maddie. It is too confusing. I used to know things. I knew when to plant corn, how to get Rocco to behave, help the cows give birth, nurse Nellie back to good health, when to plant tobacco, when it was time to eat even before you rang the dinner bell, how to level the hay wagon, fix the broken wheel, tame the colts, fatten the pigs for market, bargain with the county, argue politics with Peter Pedretti, hunt down a deer, shoot a bow and arrow into a target's heart at a hundred feet.

Most days I don't remember. On a good day I sometimes read my letters to you – they make no sense; I do not even remember writing them. I don't know where they came from. Maddie have you read them?

Today, Maddie, I know only two things. I wish you were here. I want to die.

October 24, 1899

"Giovanni, where are you? Sleeping again? Every time I come to take you, you are asleep. I can't take you in your sleep; it seems too cruel to let you go and you don't even know it."

-Madeline

It's later – maybe the same day, I don't really know. I am losing it. Did I make that entry or did Maddie come back from the dead? It is written in my handwriting, Maddie signed it. Did you come and take my hand to write this in my sleep? I don't remember writing it. I could not have written it. I don't think Lucy would write it. You wrote it. You were here. You made that entry in my handwriting. But you wrote it. I know you did. Didn't you? When you come again, and I am asleep, remove my soul, take me, please, repossess me.

November 7, 1899

"I think I could turn and live awhile with the animals....they are so placid and self-contained." WW

How can young Peter and Stephen Pedretti drop everything and hunt "the placid and self-contained"? Those two whipper-snappers will let their hay rot in the field while they hunt deer or fox or coon. I hear they even eat the coon. These are god's creatures. Leave them alone. I want to shout, "Go rake your hay and put it away for the cows. Cows are meant to be eaten, not god's "placid" animals of the forest. They are a couple of lazy good-for-nothings trying to harvest nature's crop instead of their own.

November 10, 1899

Is this the idea for the first chapter of, "Venner's Little Book of Truths"?

Every great culture has been both made and defined by its artists. If America is to ever become the great nation that it can become, there must be a creative arts renaissance. Every civilization from the smallest tribes to the most powerful nations has provided patronage for artists. Art, like parks and schools, is for the common good. To have it restricted for the benefit of the entitled is an oxymoron. The only way to assure art is made for the benefit of all is to have it subsidized by the republic.

November 11, 1899
Maddie,

Homer came last night. He was a handsome fellow. Gentle. Fatherly. Quite the opposite of Primo. He asked for you. Wanted to know about the boys. We talked. Told stories about our grandparents. Shared ideas on planting practices. Bragged on our horses. He asked about *Valle di Santa Maria Prima Della Morte.* "Will you finish it?"

I lied and said "Yes, I will return to it tomorrow. I will not let death come until the last i is dotted."

"Let it wait, Giovanni. You have a bigger task that you must do. The gods have writ that you must write the epic to straighten out the errors that I and Virgil, Milton and Dante have made. We celebrated war & quest, chauvinism, evil & despair, fear and apparitions. We left a legacy of aggressive angst, boisterous xenophobia, treacherous righteousness, and toxic terror, as if that was the way. Giovanni, you have what it takes to set it right. It is not bellicosity, jingoism, rectitude or dread that ought to have been celebrated. How did we get it so wrong?"

He paused, looked at me. "What do I know? " I asked. "I am just a farmer, a husband, a father, a son. I don't even believe in God, or gods, or fate. How can I tell of how the universe works? And I am old, not much time left, not many desires left." Homer locked his eyes on mine. Completely intimidated now, I added, "I'm not a writer."

As he was to speak, Lucy woke me up with her discordant "Good Morning, Johnneeee. Rise and shine. Come and get it"

November 12

Maddie, I can't get the words of Homer out of my mind. Are we warmongers because of Homer's words or did he write about what we are? Look at America. We came here to avoid the monstrosities of Europe – the Kings, feudalism, poverty, and most of all the wars whose destructiveness led to starvation, plagues, dependency and Kings. And yet, we cannot give up war. From the day we became a nation to the day I write this to you, we have been at war. I ask, "What are we fighting for?" We have land a plenty, people enough, independence from subjugation, a chance to make free with it. In this decade alone we have massacred our own in South Dakota, sent troops to battle in Argentina, Chile, Haiti, Nicaragua, China, Korea, Panama, Nicaragua again, China again, Nicaragua for the third time in a decade, Samoa, sent our troops against citizens in Idaho, Chicago, and now again in Idaho where we are holding workers captive in Coeur d'Alene. We attacked the independent country of Hawaii and annexed it like the covetous ogres that we are. For the umpteenth time we sent out our troops once more to battle an Indian tribe [in Minnesota this time] as if having killed 99% of them already was not enough. All of that overshadowed by our attack on Spain designed to sell newspapers and resulting in us conquering Puerto Rico, Guam, Cuba, [where we turned that good-for-nothing momma's baby Roosevelt into a candidate for vice-president] and the Philippines where we killed 600,000 Filipinos. Yes, we killed 600,000 innocent Filipinos who merely wanted their freedom from Swaggering Spain and then from Assailant America.

Maddie, I only write of this decade. I could go on and on how belligerent we were in the past. In what was probably the most unjustifiable war, we stole Texas, California, Nevada, Arizona, Utah, New Mexico and a good apart of Colorado and Wyoming from the Mexican people. I could blame the meek politicians with their acquiescence to the song of the entitled, but Polk ran openly on a platform of xenophobic and pugnacious aggression. America, you have what it takes, why are you rattling your swords, why do you insist on being the foot soldiers for Rockefeller, Vanderbilt, Astor and Girard?

November 13

The line from *I Promessi Sposi* that I memorized as a young student came back to me, "Even in the scarcest times, public money may always be found to be employed foolishly." Especially for war; always we have money for war. Even in face of the greatest plague to hit Italy, Charles V had money for war but not to help the afflicted. Are we any different?

November 14, 1899

Homer won't let me alone. He came in my dreams again – this time just his voice, "Write the Great American Epic – make it about yourself, your Tom, your Maddie, about your neighbor Peter, tell the story of Primo and especially about your grandma and her momma and her momma all the way back to the time the great valley of St. James the Greater was settled. The story of kindness is in your blood, it is before you, it is in you. You are the emancipator and it is through your story of stories that the way will be spoken. Tell the story of family, gentleness, charity, peace. You have what it takes to inspire, to get your fellow countrymen to defend man not country, to remove the marks of greed, bellicosity, selfishness, to find in themselves love which each was born with, to return to their core of charity. That core is suppressed deep in each one, you know it, and you, only you, can provide the implements for each to scrape away the scabs that have scarred their center."

Maddie, what am I to do? My hand is too unsteady, my mind too crumbled, my spirit too charred, my language too rusty, English still foreign, kindness itself clipped. Homer, leave me alone, I cannot write this story.

November 15

It is the kernel of corn
In the womb of my soil
That speaks of god.

November 16, 1899

The first step for America to discontinue engaging in war is to admit we are warmongers and not peace lovers. As long as we think we are peace givers, the public will be doped into fighting the wars of the entitled few. America has never fought a justifiable war. I dare you to show otherwise.

That is another idea for my little book. Homer, let me write the "little" book – I can do it. I am too old to write your dream epic. Why didn't you write it to begin with? Maybe one of my offspring will write it. You could appear to him, but for god's sake, help him a little more than just telling him he can do it.

[Editor's note: I believe John would have concluded that America's participation in WWII was justified].

November 16

You can't get out of life alive.

November 17, 1899
Maddie,

"I am the clock myself."

"I am afoot with my vision."

"Nor do I understand who there can be more wonderful than myself." (Nor I, Mr. Walter Whitman.)

"I know I am solid and sound,

To me the converging objects of the universe perpetually flow,

All are written to me, and I must get what the writing means."

"I know I am august,

I do not trouble my spirit to vindicate itself or be understood,

I see that the elementary laws never apologize"
"I am the poet of the body
I am the poet of the Soul." –WW

Master Walt, I, John Venner, am the body and the soul. I, John Venner, am Walter and Thomas and George and Benjamin. I have it in me. I am august. I am the wind and the corn. Walter, you have nothing on me. I come from the people; I am the people, it is me. The pleasures of heaven are with me, the pains of hell are with me. I am Abraham. I, who can make a corn stalk from a kernel, wheat fields from a bushel of leftover grain; I am greater than them all. I was meant to be poetizer of our time. My mother before me; my children after me; we are the eagle.

Walt, it is I who is the joy of heaven; I am the pain of hell. It is only through me that you can understand who you are, what you have become. I would have written the story of all stories but for the fate of being born in a barren place and escaping to Bad Ax. Bad Ax of all places. In this loony bin or not, I will write the poem you never could write, for it is I that have witnessed the morning sun, I who have fertilized the dream, weeded evil out; I am America, I am the harvest and the leaf and the rock, Sisyphus, Isis and Aphrodite.

After Walt

Born behind
Time
Just beyond
Bad Ax City

He lusted for the leafs
And twigs and branches
Her love, the creek, the book of poems,
The roots, and he ate
Them all.
Apple too.

Behind this man
There are so many what-could-have-beens
He has suppressed mankind's failures
Into a single lifetime.

So I'm a little rusty. Walt, what if you never wrote for fifty years? I had a wife to care for; kids to raise, a frontier to conquer. OK, it is no excuse, but it is my defense. I will write every day now, Walt, and you will see, I am a better poet than you – than you even dreamed of becoming. It is my voice that America will listen to.

November 18

This hellhole is just that. They take everything. I asked the nurse for a knife. She laughed. I thought I could get my head in between the bars on the window. I could pull it off. I still have the strength, I know I have. But no use, the bastards put the bars too close. I thought about pounding my head against the wall; but I know they'd hear me and stop me before the job was done.

"I hasten to inform him or her it is just as lucky to die, and I know it." Whitman don't know fuck about dying. But he is right, if I could just be so lucky as to die. "Has any one supposed it lucky to be born?" Not me Walt, not me. For you, yes, you were born right. "They are alive and well somewhere." I'm alive, Walt, but nothing well about it. Nothing well about it at all. And as to you, Death, where are you and your rapt hug of mortality? It is idle to try to alarm me. It is lucky to die, and I know it. "Death is welcome." Come now. I am ready. I yearn for you.

November 19, 1899

I been thinking about Grandma - and Campodolcino. The Valley of St. James. Oh Grandma, you were an angel. Not because you lived with Giacomo or were my grandma. Not because you died of exhaustion at age 58. For those sacrifices you should be canonized. No I mean a saint as in a brave loving person who had strong beliefs grounded in kindness and who acted with passion.

Before I got on that boat, I began to write your story. A novel that would rival *I Promessi Sposi*. I thought I would finish your story while I rode the Atlantic Ocean from the ports of La Havre to the New York Harbor – the long journey with no responsibilities for the first time in my life. The clear sky and water to inspire me, the quiet to let the story come. But no – each day was a struggle to stay alive. The sickness hit us hard. Frank was lost. He could hold nothing down. For days he lingered, barely breathing. I never left his side except to get water to bathe him. On the seventh day his eyes opened, and I was able to nurse him back only to get the sickness too. I knew I would die, for nine out of ten were dying. Frank had survived – my chances diminished to zero. I said my goodbyes and drifted off into blackness. Frank told me I was gone for five days, then to everyone's surprise, I too recovered. It took three more days to get out of bed and another week before I could get up the stairs to the deck. Forty days and forty nights after we departed France we beheld New York. Only 42 of us made the trip, but I don't think the captain gave a shit. Everyone had to pay for the trip before boarding – getting us there did not seem to be his concern. Collecting the fee and docking his boat mattered.

We spent two days getting through customs, were told the train to Chicago was not ready, found a coach heading to Cleveland, boarded it, and when we got to Cleveland, Frank and I pooled our money to buy two tickets to Chicago. We would arrive, maybe 200 miles from our destination, without a lira to our name. What to do? Finally luck came our way. On board was John Gianoli who told us he was being met in Chicago by his uncle. We could ride to Bad Ax with them and pay him back for food after we got established. The ride was rough and food scarce – but it was a piece of cake compared to the ride we'd had on Charon's boat.

My body got to Bad Ax; that is, it barely got there. I was sick with the fever. Frank was in no better shape. We asked for Albert Zaboglio. We went to his house; he said he couldn't help – we looked like the plague warmed over and he could not take a chance we might infect his family. He said a friend owned a shack just outside of town. We could stay there. He'd tell his friend we were there. "Wait" he said and went into his house and came back with a sack stuffed with food. We drug it in the direction he told us. We had no trouble finding the shack. We had not eaten in two days, so we tore open the sack and found a loaf of bread – disgusting soft gooey stuff, but we ate it till we were full and then lay on the floor and slept I don't know how long. Primo appeared in my dreams – it was the first time I remember when his head was two times what it was. Accused me of abandoning him in his old age. He had abandoned me the day I was born. He had abandoned himself to grappa before I was born. How could I abandon him? In his old age? He was only 63, ok he looked a warmed over 90, but that was the booze. When I woke I was soaked. It was bright out. Frank was gone. I did not know where I was, how I had gotten there, where Frank was. I knew that I had made the greatest mistake in my life leaving the land of my momma and the coziness of Campodolcino to travel across the ocean to this godforsaken place. I yelled for Frank, he came in with a bucket of water he had collected from the creek running not too far from the shack. I drank some, sloshed some on my forehead. I never felt anything so good. For the next week Frank took care of me. He was sickly too, but I guess I was worse. We managed with the cool, fresh water from the creek and the sack of Zaboglio food. Finally I felt strong enough to walk back into Bad Ax. We ran into Sister Beffa and Guglielmo Pedretti on the street. Everything felt so strange, yet so familiar. The river was too large, the mountains too short, the valley too green, the people too mean. But still there were mountains and water and a valley and faces we had known in Campodolcino. Frank got a job working for Anthony Levi, and I talked Bart Penchi into hiring me to work in his lumberyard. Nobody had any money to pay for work. Frank made 50 cents a day and I got paid in trade that Penchi had received and could not use for his family. I got paid a lot of eggs, I have not been able to eat an egg since – to this day – 45 years later - I still can't stand to look at an egg, let alone eat one.

I just got called to dinner. I'll write some more this afternoon.

Dinner was barely fit for the pigs. Where do they even find such crap? We are in the heart of the greatest fresh food available in any place in the world, but the best they can do is give us cold stale food that must be a week or more old.

Grandma, I been remembering the story I started to write about the woman you could have been; the woman you could have been if you had not married Primo, had lived in another place and time. But the story kept coming back to a woman full of promise, who suffers one loss after another until there is nothing left but death. It is not the story I wanted to write, but it kept writing itself. I wanted to celebrate what could have been, but the muse spoke of what was; of seven losses. I wish I could find the manuscript. Maybe it is in the attic. Tom's living there now; I'll ask him to look. I think I can write the story.

Thanksgiving Day 11/23/99

[Dearest Reader, John recorded a particularly bad day. It is best I spare you reading about the depths his spirit reached as he felt there was less than even nothing to be thankful about].

November 24, 1899

Maddie, I did not write more. It is hard- this writing business. Even to write to you in this diary, it is hard. No wonder I never finished the book about Grandma. I been trying to remember what happened to the part I had written. I know I took them on the boat. I remembered easily enough that I had them when I got off the boat. But everything was so blurry about the trip to Bad Ax and being so sick. I could not remember if I had the story in that shack Frank and I lived in for our first three years in Bad Ax. Then it came to me. I remembered picking it up one cool summer evening and taking it over to the creek and dipping my sore bare feet into the still cold running water and opening up the manuscript and reading it. I could see my grandma on every page. I had her, I thought. She is alive and real. I got to finish this book. Why didn't I? I have no excuse. I know they say if you are a writer you have to write. I don't believe it. For every Dante that has the good fortune to be able to write, there are 100 Dantes that for whatever reason never see their work make it into the public's conscience. Maybe they never find the time, take the time, believe in themselves, find a publisher, have anyone believe in them, never find the reader. I don't know, but it makes them not one iota less able to write the great epic of their time than Dante.

Could I still write the book? That is a question. That is the question.

But now I knew I had the book after I arrived in Bad Ax. What happened to it? I just cannot remember. Next time Tom comes, I'll ask him to look for it in the attic. Must be where it is. If he can't find it, maybe I can write it again. Can I even remember what I wrote? I should write it down – maybe tomorrow. Tired now.

December 2

"I got it wrong John – it is not about which nation you live in, but which body you live in."

-Publius Vergilius Maro [aka Virgil]

December 5, 1899

Dearest Maddie,

The nurse told me I was lucky today. "You having a good day. Enjoy it" she said to me. My favorite thing to do is to write to you.

Maddie, I have that dream about my old man every night. I hate that dream. I guess Primo was a good man, but I was too afraid of him to see that. Even in the daytime that moment in the dream comes back, the one where I cannot kiss him. How could I? I had forgotten. Forgotten how that man used to beat me to a pulp. How I made myself breathe to bear the pain. How I would stare into the ceiling to forget. I watch myself horizontal with no emotion. Still Primo was harder on Giacomo, and I always felt a little lucky. Every night I wake out of this dream sweating like a pig.

I want to let this man who created so much anger in me go to hell where he belongs. I can't. He has come back. Only you made him go away. You, with your touch, your smile, your love for life; you kept him at bay. But now you are gone and he is back. He is gripping my soul. Primo, leave me, please.

It was nine months today you left me, Maddie. That's long enough. If a baby can be born in nine months, why can't a husband join his wife in nine months? Jesus I am ready, let me unite with Maddie, slip me through the gate into the new life there. I traveled from Prestone to Bad Ax. Now I'm ready to travel from Viroqua to be with you and with my Maddie.

I can go no more. There is nothing no more. I must sleep forever.

December 6, 1899

They let me out today. The sun was shining. The snow is gone. The wind was blowing. The sky grayish blue just like that day I boarded the boat in Havre. My sister was with me. She was crying. I asked her to come with me. I said, "Marta, you don't need to go back to Prestone to Primo who is only first in being mean. Come with me, I will take care of you. We will find a new life. I will care for you". I bought her a ticket, one way from Havre to New York. She had a hundred excuses, Primo needed her, he would starve without her, she did not pack her belongings, she needed more clothes, the Indians were too scary, the priest was expecting her to lead the rosary next week, and on and on and on some more. But all the time she clung to that ticket and walked with me to the boat. I thought for a moment she was coming. But in the end her obligations overcame her desire to make free with it. She hugged me, turned and ran to the furthermost livery. Marta my sister, I miss you. Maddie, my heart broke that day and ached to the day I married you.

December 9, 1899

Two more ideas for the Venners' *Book of Truths*:

We bandy about the terms conservative and liberal. These terms are the creation of the entitled. They have no meaning. The political discourse is about the rights of the entitled versus the rights of the citizen – takers versus givers. By substituting the terms conservative and liberal, the entitled obscure their role as belligerent assailants and cloak their insatiability in respectable cloths and the disenfranchised are marginalized and alienated.

No American man should receive more than 12 times the income of the least well paid person in America. If the greedy take more, they are to face hard time; so severe, that the rich will err on the side of less and not take more than 11 times – call that the "Venner dozen" - for fear of punishment will keep the entitled on the safe side. Bakers' Dozen? – I say better a Venner Dozen.

December 10, 1899
Good Morning, Maddie,

I been reading Whitman again: "Nor do I understand who there can be more wonderful than myself." Shit, I hear the lady coming to take us for a walk – I promise I will write to you when I get back.

It's a few hours later now – I just read:

> "The farmer stops by the bars as he walks on a first-
> day loafe and
> looks at the oats and rye,
> The lunatic is carried at last to the asylum a confirm'd
> case"

Walt, the farmer and the lunatic, they are one and the same, they are me. Maybe you have to be a lunatic to be a farmer. Maybe you have to be a farmer to be a lunatic. How else can one work from dawn to past dusk, knowing that the work he makes is the most important to the survival of our countrymen, for the wages a banker makes in half an hour? The wonder is not that I am here, but that I avoided the place for so many years. Yes, the farmer and the lunatic, they are one and the same.

"Nor do I understand who there can be more grotesque than myself."

Ah, yes. Enough said for today.

December 12, 1899

Tom came today. I asked him why Rocco and Ursula put me in this nut place. He claimed they'd found me in my garden humming and gently hoeing our tomato patch; hoeing out not the weeds but the tomato plants. I told him he was the crazy one; no way would this farmer hoe out one tomato let alone all of them. I remember now - I was knocking the ripe tomatoes on the ground, smashing the blood out of them, then hoeing out one plant after another. I would whack one from the left, the next one from the right and then one straight on. I was making up a poem. I don't remember it now, but it went something like

This ole tomato took my Maddie,
This ole tomato took none
This ole tomato ain't going to market

This ole tomato is going to pay
This ole tomato better wee-wee on the ground
Or I'll hoe, hoe, hoe them all down.

Tom said I'd already cut all the peas and beans off. I don't think so. You know what our garden meant to me. Tomatoes, sure. I could see myself cutting them out. I never liked a tomato and you loved them. They reminded me of you. He took you, I would take the tomatoes. But not the beans and peas. No way. I remember now, Tom and Ursula came over. I remember Ursula staring at me. I said hi, she said nothing. Tom approached me, said hello, slid his hand over the hoe and pulled it away from me as if he was disarming me. He took my arm, said "Come on Dad" and took me toward the front door of the house. I sat in the front yard. I recall it was a nice day.

Rocco came over. I heard them talking, like I wasn't there, about how batty I was. Rocco said better take him to Viroqua, Ursula said no, maybe the heat got to him. Rocco said, "Think the heat got to him yesterday? And the day before? And the day before that? It ain't the heat Urse, it's the brains." Ursula said, "Let's just take all the guns and knives. He'll be fine if we can keep the dangerous things away and check on him every day."

Maybe the heat had gotten to me. But for sure my children were getting to me. I can't imagine Giacomo and me talking about our dad like that, no matter how bad he got. No matter how old we were, he would'a beat our butts good.

Tom said he was sorry, that he did not know what else to do, and then he left.

December 13, 1899

> "I am of old and young, of the foolish as much as the
> wise...
>
> A farmer, mechanic, or artist.... A gentleman, sailor,
> lover or Quaker,
>
> A prisoner, fancy-man, rowdy, lawyer, physician or
> priest."

I know Whitman is saying that he is of each of these, each is as valuable as the other, but I can't help notice the order in which he lists these people.

A. "A farmer, mechanic, or artist" – each in his own way a creator. The farmer making food from seed for our body, the mechanic making the tools we need and repairing the broken, the artist making food for our soul from his imagination.

B. "A gentleman, sailor, lover or Quaker," - each in his own way giving more than taking.

C. "A prisoner, fancy-man, rowdy, lawyer, physician or priest." Each in his own way taking more than giving – and I think in the order that they take. The prisoner taking our money, the fancy-man our dignity, the rowdy our self-respect, the lawyer our freedom, the physician our life and the priest our soul.

[Editor: In his next entry, John tells Maddie that his nightmare with his father, Primo, has stopped. He begins to write daily, his wishes vacillate between wanting to return to the farm and join Maddie in death. Walt Whitman dominates his thoughts. He scribbles notes for poems he never writes; convinced he could have been the Dante of America. There is no mention of Christmas or the arrival of a new century.]

January 22, 1900

Bessie's dead. Best cow I ever had. She's gone. Tom came by to tell me. He is a good son. I remember the day I got her. It must have been 15 - 20 years ago when young Peter Pedretti set out to Ames, Iowa to buy some Holstein cows and the best bull he could buy. I told him, "Just bring me one cow; the very best one they put up for sale." If Peter got the best bull and I got the best cow, I know I could make a herd. And we did. Yes Maddie, we did. No one this side of the Mississippi has a better herd of milking cows than Madeline and Giovanni Venner. And Bessie was momma and grandmother to the best of them.

January 23, 1900

There are three basic political systems – democracy, republic, totalitarian. There are three basic economic systems – communism, socialism and capitalism. They go together like this:

- o Communism & Democracy = everyone shares equal wealth and power
- o Socialism and Republic = each granted wealth and power according to his or her ability and contribution to society.
- o Capitalism and Totalitarianism = wealth and power go to the strongest or at least the greediest.

We have had small democratic communistic societies. We have had totalitarian capitalistic regimes. We have had a variety of mixed forms [e.g. Totalitarian communist regimes]. None has worked. The best government and economic system would be a democratic socialist republic.

It is what we had in Val San Giacomo for about 700 years and it worked beautifully. Please note – I could develop this idea and make it one of our ten little truths.

Please note: Capitalism's claim that America's growth is due to its system cannot be documented, and any economist worth his salt should be able to demonstrate that we have had growth despite and not because of capitalism. America's success as a nation of wealth is not due to capitalism but to abundant natural resources (safeguarded for centuries by Indians), free public education and a strong talented labor force. [Got to develop this fact]

January 24, 1900

Here is another truth to develop for another chapter in "The Venner Book of Truths."

We need a new religion based on the fact that we are each responsible to make the most of our span of 3 score and ten years or so. I believe in the next 50 years a prophet will emerge to provide a new moral code providing the understanding of the centrality of charity and the necessity to be ruled by the principle of kindness. This may sound like an oxymoron, but we need a Founder of Disbelief. To put it in another way, we desperately need a founder of the Church of Kindness, the Church of Joy.

And another truth!

Standardization of our educational system will weaken and possibly destroy the third leg in our economic system.

January 27
Maddie,

The great John Milton came last night. He towered over me like Death shadows our every waking hour. His singing rang through my vision with thundering clarity, "Eve knew." "Eve knew" echoed through my dream for what seemed like hours until the mountain behind exploded into a nightmare of covetous men wallowing in their own excrements, narcissistic women splitting into seventeen shafts, authoritarian repressors expanding into an eruption triggered by the blood of their victims.

Milton's shadow covered the earth and his voice blew across the Atlantic, "Eve knew not eating Death." Over and over, the nightmare repeated itself.

Today I tried to parse the sentence, "Eve knew; not eating death." Or "Eve knew not; eating death." Or could it be, "Eve knew not eating – death." Or simply "Eve, knew not."

Milton, leave me alone. Charles II should have hung you.

January 28
Milton came again. Went on about how Eve did not bring us death. "Death always existed," he said. "By eating of

the tree of knowledge, she made us aware that death was coming; leaving us with the need to invent god, to seek meaning where there may not be any, to listen to the prophesies of madmen for their ravings gave more solace than uncertainty. By eating of knowledge she forsook innocence, making ignorance possible, crime probable, and death predictable. "

What the hell was he talking about?

January 31, 1900

The Milton nightmares led me to think about evil. The crimes of our time are made in the name of democracy. It is the wealthy and the powerful that suffocate the rest. The seven vices include avarice and greed, but none speaks to the worst vice of all – the lust for power. In fact I cannot think of a word that describes the evil of 'power accumulation' that would parallel to lust, greed, avarice, pride etc. I guess Evagrius and Gregory were themselves sinners of power-hungriness and therefore were not so interested in identifying their compulsion as a vice.

February 8, 1900

Maddie,

Primo came back last night. This time his face was bigger than the bedroom wall and it screamed over and over, "How could you leave me?" I clapped my hands over my ears, but the voice shouted louder. I closed my eyes, but the face got brighter.

"Stop it! Stop it! Stop it!" I murmured.

But the voice got louder and the face bigger. I screamed

at the top of my lungs. His voice stopped and the face faded. I screamed louder as if to chase away this horror.

I saw a white figure in the brightness. I sighed a moment of relief as I thought it was the Angel of Afterlife coming to get me.

"You alright, John?" How did she know my name was John? It had to be the Angel.

"John, you alright? Do you know where you are? It's okay. You'll be all right. You been here three months now. It's okay. We'll help you get better. Remember me? I'm Lucy. Remember? You're in Vernon County Asylum. Remember? We're going to make you better. There is nothing to be afraid of. Come on now. Let's lie back down and get some sleepy-bye. Okay. It's all right. Lucy will protect you. No problem. Just lie down and get some sleep. The bogeyman wouldn't come. Now, now. There you go. I'll just pull these covers up and tuck them in. Just close your eyes and go to sleep now. It's okay. I'll just turn the lights out. Beddie-bye. Sleep tight."

The apparition was gone. It was pitch dark. Where was the light from the street? Did someone close my shade? I reached over the left side of my bed and ran my hand across the wall toward the window. But there was only the wall. Who took out the window? I noticed a bit of light coming from under the door. "Who had the light on in the kitchen?" I wondered. I lay back in the bed. The room began to spin out of control. I closed my hands over my ears, tried to go to sleep, but the room spun and spun and spun.

February 9, 1900

I think a spider climbed in my eye last night. There are

webs in my eyes and my brain sleeps as my head nods onto the paper I am writing on. My eyes have seen the coming and the glory of the aurora. The waterfall is made of fire.

February 12, 1900

> All the men ever born are also my brothers....and the women my sisters and lovers" - Walt Whitman

February 14, 1900 – A full moon tonight

Lauds [Dawn]

John, let us hold hands and give thanks. Born of Primo and Margarita, we suffered his angst and joyed in her love. When she abandoned us in death before her time, we resolved to join our friends in America, but the war set us back and a decade passed before we had enough lire to get here. Sickness sucked the adventure out of our trip, but we made it, we recovered. We married well, sired strong healthy children and turned our farms into little paradises of fertility.

John, let us lift our eyes to heaven and give thanks for a life more blessed than was possible to even imagine while living in the shadow of Pizzo Stella and Primo Vener.

My wife and I been reading the psalms. I think you will like this section from 149:

> Let them praise his name with dancing
> and make music to him with timbrel and harp.
> For the LORD takes delight in his people;
> he crowns the humble with victory.

Let his faithful people rejoice in this honor
and sing for joy on their beds.

Your brother,
Frank Vener [Hey John, notice I did not add an "n" to
our name.]

Prime (6AM)

Deus in adjutorium
Bring us love [love I say]
Bring us peace [peace I say]
Bring us joy [joy, joy, joy]

The Song:
Love, according to Webster:
To hold dear
Cherish
To feel a lover's passion, devotion, or tenderness for
Caress
To fondle amorously
To copulate with
To like or to desire actively
Take pleasure in
To thrive in
To feel affection or experience desire

The Psalm: [substitute]
And be ye kind one to another, tenderhearted, forgiving
one another, even as God for Christ's sake hath forgiven you. -
Ephesians 4:32

The Lesson:

My Johnny, you gave meaning to my waking hours. To look into your eyes was to feel joy. To romp about the woods together looking for walnuts and hickory nuts was to know God. To sleep with you was to become warmth. Never did a day pass without a prayer of thanks that you entered my life.

The Response:

Maddie, I only ever woke because you were there.

The Versicle:

With thee conversing I forget all time,
All seasons and their change, all please alike.
Sweet is the breath of morn, her rising sweet,
With charm of earliest birds; pleasant the sun
When first on this delightful land he spreads
His orient beams, on herb, tree, fruit, and flower,
Glistening with dew; fragrant the fertile earth
After soft shower; and sweet the coming on
Of grateful evening mild, then silent night – John
    Milton

Love conquers all things; let us too surrender to Love.
    -Virgil

The Kyrie:

The Lord gave us life. He will take it at his will, not
    yours.

The Pater:

> Our Father who lights the heaven
> May John rest with you and with me.

The Oratio:

> "The unjust and oppressive, all those, in fact, who wrong others, are guilty, not only of the evil they do, but also of the perversion of mind they cause in those whom they offend." –Alessandro Manzoni

The Prayer:

> Oh my Johnny, Your time is not yet. Finish your work and death will come to fetch you from your hurt.

> Love,
> Maddie

Terce (9 AM)

Father, I stand before you humbled by the size of your life. Each day brings its own struggle with rain on the hay, a lost cow in childbirth, blighted corn field, feathers of the fox-eaten chicken, fields turned into roads, fifteen hour days, broken fences, moldy silage, depressed milk prices -- What are they compared to immigrating, lost child, lost wife, lost mind?

> Your loving son,
> -Tom

Sext (Noon)

> Deus in adjutorium:
> Come and listen children (come and listen children),
> listen to the story (listen to the story)
> I'm going to sing it, shout it, tell it all of my days (yes,
> all of my days)

The Song:

> This is the story
> The story of my people
> Listen
> I sing no more
> For the story
> Is told.

The Psalm: [118]:

> With the holy you will be holy; and with the innocent
> man you will be innocent:
> And with the elect you will be elect: and with the
> perverse you will be perverted.
> For you will save the humble people; but will bring
> down the eyes of the proud.
> For you light my lamp

The Lesson:

I speak now to my grandson or great grandson who will stumble upon this book. You, oh Curious One, you must write the stories I never wrote – the story of Grandma, the story of our stories tracing us from the beginning of the Valley of Saint James to your own time and maybe beyond. My story, yes tell them my story for herein….. [Editor: the entry stopped abruptly]

The Response:
>   Grandfather of mine, who are you? Where are you? I have your words, but you escape me.

The Versicle:
>   Whitman
>>   Speech is the twin of my vision….it is unequal to measure itself.
>>   It provokes me forever,
>>   It says sarcastically, Walt, you understand enough…. why don't you let it out then? -WW

>   We ought to aim rather at doing well, than being well.
>   -Manzoni

The Oratio:
>   Grandpa Giovanni of the Valley of Saint James, bring me your wisdom, courage, and creativity to make what you have dreamed into words that remember your revelation. I will be your archangel.

Prayer:
>   Grandfather of mine, who are you? Where are you? I have your words, but you escape me.
>>   -Your Great Grandchild Gabriel Michael Raphael Uriel Phanuel Zarachiel Simiel

None (3PM)

"John! John!" my head was inside a megaphone, the voice screaming at me. "You worthless tit. You good-for-nothing no count piece of shit balled up in a cup of cow piss. You ain't worth the teats on a boar. From the moment you were born I knew you would amount to nothing. Oh you were going to write the great epic about your mother. You wrote nothing – hot air, that's what you are. Best you could do was desert your mother when she needed you most. Left her lying in bed dying while you caroused with your friends. You were her poison. All she wanted was to turn you into something. Fat chance. When you got out of her life, she got her life back. Too late for me, I was already dead. But I watched. You think you are dead when you are dead, but it ain't true. I was there watching you destroy my wife. I was there on the boat with your great America – leave your country, your mother your friends behind to go adventuring in some god forsaken wilderness. You deserved every pain you ever got, every loss that came your way, every disappointment that defined your life. You are a worthless two-bit good for nothing. -Primo

What's happening? Maddie, help me. I can't get up. Please. It's afternoon. The monsters won't leave. I am a wreck. My right cheek is numb. Help. Pray with me.

> Lord, now lettest thou thy servant depart in peace according to thy word.

For mine eyes

[Editor: the writing stopped with the s spreading across the page as if the writer fell asleep as he was finishing the word.]

Vespers (Sunset)

Giovanni, I love you. I am distraught to see you locked in a cell like a common criminal. What's with America? What's with your children? Is this why I gave you birth? Is this why I nurtured your inquisitiveness? Why I told you to run with your friends even though I knew I was dying? Oh John, where did our dreams go? I know I abandoned you to your father. But I could not go on. I don't know if it was the fever or lost hope that got me. For you I wanted to live, but there was no more will.

My dear Giovanni, you were a gifted writer. I stood over you and read every word you wrote. I was both touched and flattered. Your insight to life and to what I was thinking was chilling. I think you still got it. But let my story go. Write the story about a family of planters, nurturers and harvesters – We have celebrated wars and warriors for too long. It is time to celebrate peace and benevolence. It is time to celebrate creativity and planting. -Momma

The Song:

> Sing, my Giovanni,
> Sing!
> The time is now.

The Psalm: [85]

> Lead us to an inner life in which we can rejoice.

Speak peace to us, that we may live in peace.
May your mercy and truth meet together
Righteousness and peace kiss each other,
Surrounding us with your light
Help us know true prosperity,
And be gentle with your Earth.
Guide our feet in the ways of peace.

The Lesson:

Momma, who are you? Where are you? I have your
memory, but you escape me.

The Response:

You will hardly know who I am or what I mean...

Failing to fetch me at first keep encouraged
Missing me one place search another
I stop some where waiting for you. -WW

Versicle:

Statement:

Man, so long as he is in this world, is like a sick person
lying upon a bed more or less uncomfortable,
who sees around him other beds nicely made to
outward appearance, smooth, and level, and
fancies that they must be most comfortable
resting-places. He succeeds in making an
exchange; but scarcely is he placed in another,
before he begins, as he presses it down, to feel in
one place a sharp point pricking him, in another a

hard lump: in short , we come to almost the same story over again.[– Manzoni, p378]

Response:

My voice goes after what my eyes cannot reach. –WW

The Prayer:

We also ascend dazzling and tremendous as the sun,
We found our own my soul in the calm and cool of the daybreak. [Walt Whitman p. 50]

Love you more,
Momma

9:00 PM-Compline

Deus in adjutorium:

Ciao Johnny, it's your best friend Nick. It is time to let go, to struggle no more, to join Maddie in peace and quiet.

The Poem:

Behold, how good and how pleasant it is for brethren to dwell together in unity! It is like the precious ointment upon the head. [Psalm 133]

The Song:

When ye pray,
Use not vain repetitions,
As the heathen [do]:
For they think that they shall be heard for their much speaking. [Matthew 6:7]

The Lesson:

Nick, I have few regrets. I made a satisfying place for my children to grow up. I had a good life with Maddie. I was true to my word. Still, there is a deep emptiness. I never told my grandma's story. I never wrote the epic of kindness. I must wake. It can still be done.

The Response:

No, Johnny. It's time to let go. You cannot save the world from itself any more than you could save your momma from Primo, Maria Angela from the measles, your namesake from the fever, Bessie from old age, Nellie from so many still births, Rocco from the bottle, Maddie from the doctors, not even your own mind from despair. I've watched you struggle with every moment. Now let it go.

The Canticle:

> Lord, now lettest thou thy servant depart in peace,
> according to thy word
> For mine eyes have seen the salvation,
> Which thou hast prepared before the face of all people.
> [Luke 2:29-31]

The Prayer:

You have graced this planet with your passion and compassion, love, labor, kindness, commitment to your family, creative spirit, faithfulness to your friends, struggle for justice, fairness in all actions, courage to confront injustice, love of peace, sensibility and sensitiveness for nigh on 70 years. Back in Campodolcino, I watched you work 16 hour days in the salt mines and save every penny to get you and Frank out of that hellhole on Contreda Street. I know, oh so well, how you almost died in Ghelfi's shack, slaved over Penchi's saw to make enough to buy Baritani's farm and pay for the patent granted by Grover Cleveland for 80 acres in section 27, to turn patch after patch of wooded land into fields, lifting bundles of hay bigger than you were, milking 30 cows every morning and evening, starting too many days at 5:00 AM and finishing them as the bats came out of hiding, fathering ten children with love, never taking a rainy day off but instead fixing this tool or that thing around the house, staying with your mares in birth, walking behind the plow through drizzle, dinner, pain, even a bad knee one year, cutting and splitting six cords of wood to get through each winter, never giving in to any challenge, the deepest despair or the cruelest bad luck. I watched you stand day and night by Maddie after you lost your two-year old angel, Marie Angela, to the measles for seven weeks until little John Baptist was born. I was there four months later with you when your namesake died and I watched you conceal your pain to once again support Maddie through her pain and loss.

Oratorio:

As Manzoni so aptly wrote, "Sorrow, I venture to say, is mingled, more or less, with everything."

Benediction:

It is time to abandon the struggle. Maddie is gone. Tom can work the farm, Rocco will find himself, Mary Ann has given Bill and Angie a home, Jake is already on his own, Ursula is a gem in a world of brittle rocks. That epic momma wants you to write – leave it for another – maybe one of your progeny will craft it out of your love and wisdom that seeps down to them. Go, Johnny, go to the other side whether it is to Maddie's heaven or to your nothingness. Take with you the knowledge that you gave it your all and you left behind a world a little bit better and your children tens of times better than you had. Fear not for what you have not completed.

Come on Johnny, this is Nick, your friend. I know where you have been, what you faced, how you pushed through time after time, your lost dreams, your accomplishments.

Go, be with Marie Angela, play with John Baptist Jr., join again with Maddie. She was young when she decided to join her maker.

-Your best friend, John Nichelatti

[Editor's note: The next entry was not dated, but appears to have been written on February 15 or 16, 1900]

Maddie,

Nightmares from death. They will not stop. It is awful, Dante's Inferno. First Frank, then you and dad and some sassy-ass from the future and Nichelatti and I don't remember who all appeared. I am soaked and exhausted. I cannot get up. I cannot sleep or eat or see. I must rest.

It's later now, I don't know how much later. Lucy, the nurse, gave me something – It made me sleep more. When I finally woke, the room was beginning to get light. Was it tomorrow or the next day? I wanted to get up, get away from the horrible dreams I had. My body would not move. I struggled up - sat on the side of the bed until I had enough strength to get up. Such nightmares I have never had. Intense. Distorted. Possessive. Frank, Tom, Momma, you, Primo, Nick, praying and singing and reading psalms. So vivid I can still see you and hear you.

Maddie, now this is scary, when I opened my diary there were messages from everyone. In my handwriting, but I did not write them. Signed by Primo, Nick, you, even one from Momma– all in my handwriting but I did not write them. How could I have written them? I was sleeping. Even if I was awake, I don't remember those psalms. I know we had to memorize some of them in Latin for the priest, but I don't remember them. I could not write them in English. Still there is no way you wrote them – you are all dead. I read them, reread them and read them again. I am frightened. What is happening? Oh my god, have I really lost it? Am I nuts like they claim; am I the Deranged Dago of the Viroqua County Asylum for the Forever Insane?

February 20, 1900

> "A child said, what is the grass? Fetching it to me with
> full hands;
> How could I answer the child?   -WW

February 22, 1900

There is more talk about that fool Roosevelt for vice-president. Some idiots even want him to replace McKinley on the ticket. He is nothing more than a warmonger. We love our wars. Americans love their war heroes. Will we ever grow up? Don't we ever learn? This country has been at war since it was founded. We can't resist a general who gets it in his head he wants to be President. Only general ever made a good president was the first one. And he needed Madison and Jefferson to keep him from completely favoring the gentry. I read not too long ago that in the last century America engaged in over 100 wars. One Hundred wars!!! Not the one hundred years' war, but the One Hundred Wars. My god, my people, what is it that you were thinking? My only hope is as we go into a new century our leaders will devote as much time, energy and money to avoiding wars as they have spent on engaging in war. The soul of every dead soldier, every dead citizen, of every dead child killed by our wars is upon our soul. We cannot escape responsibility.

February 27, 1900

From my Walt to my Nellie:

"What is it that you express in your eyes?
It seems to me more than all the print I have read in my life." –WW

It is a leap year. There will be no tomorrow for, I am told, that the day after today will be March 1. There will be no February 29. A coyote trick of the calendar. Tomorrow will never come as it will be replaced by the day after tomorrow.

And the Chaste Moon will be full. Beware.

March 1, 1900

    I had a dream last night about Abraham and his God. Not the gods of Abraham but the God of Abraham, a god so full of pride he wanted Abraham and his followers to only worship him; to have no false gods worshipped before him. I observed Abraham, standing in the light of a full Moon of the Wind, speak to his people, "I had a dream and in my dream YHWH, our god of guilt and revenge, came to me and said, 'Abraham, I am to be your god, the god of your people, the god of my people. No more are you to make sacrifice to other gods, you are to worship only me. Use your sheep and your harvest to feed your people, use your brick to make homes for your people. Squander none of it on false gods. I am your God, believe in me, preserve your sons and daughters to multiply and your produce and animals to feed my people. Make me your one and only God and you will become a great people for I will protect you from your enemies."

    In my dream I asked Abraham, "Why make one god? And, why did you make this god so demanding, so full of rage, so self-centered?"

    Abraham spoke to me, "The Babylonians have many gods. The Egyptians have many gods. The people of Sumer have many gods. We too had many gods. Each god must be worshipped. Each god demands sacrifices. This god demands prayers, that one a lamb, others the best of the harvest, some demand human sacrifice. Egypt is big, they have the Nile, and there are many people. Babylonia has much land, they too have rivers supplying water and rich soil, and they have many sheep and people. My people are not many, we live between two powerful peoples, we eke our living from the desert. We do not need many gods. We have not enough lambs. An omnipotent god who can fuse us into one people who can combat or escape the assaults of our neighbors is enough for us. His wrath is reserved for when our people stray from his teachings, when they stray from being one people. Only by being one people and only by living in fear of the wrath of God can we stay alert and ready to defend ourselves from powerful enemies."

And so Abraham declared to his people that henceforth there was only one God and his people, being of one mind and seeing the advantages of one god, praised this new god and declared themselves to be his people and pledged that they would no longer offer sacrifice to any other god before this time. The people praised Abraham for his wisdom and made sacrifice to their god, yielding to him the fruit of their harvest.

March 2, 1900

March 2, 1877 4:10 AM. The time will live forever in ignominy. For 24 years I have mourned for America and for democracy. It was a scandalous day. I don't remember much anymore, but I remember exactly where I was standing when the news arrived that the winner lost and the loser won. It was a dark day for America. I voted for Hayes. Tilden was a first class bigot and I could not understand how anyone could vote for a man who proclaimed he was of a superior race. I thought he'd get five votes, his own and his wife's, Hendricks and his wife, and their campaign manager. But he got a clear majority – even got a majority of electoral votes. It was a sad day in America when the commission voted straight party lines and placed the loser in the White House. Not only did senators and representatives vote party lines; the five commissioners from the Supreme Court ignored the law in favor of partisanship. May our country never have its future placed in the hands of a biased Supreme Court. They have proven themselves sinners and there is no reason the future promises a deliberate decision.

March 3, 1900

There is no lilac in America anymore.

March 4, 1900

Abraham came back last night. This time he was on top of Mt. Moriah with Isaac in one hand and a sword in the other. Maddie was at his side. "What are you doing?" she asked incredulously. She screamed, "Don't do it."

"I must," he said, "for my God and my people have demanded it." He explained to her that a great drought had come upon his people. "My people sacrificed extra lambs to our God. No rain. I burnt our best grain in his honor, still no rain. On the holy day of burning a virgin, we burned three virgins. Still no rain.

"My people looked to me and demanded that I sacrifice my true heir, for they knew that the only way to appease a truly angry god was for the king to sacrifice his eldest son. Needing time, I said, 'The omens are not good, we must not sacrifice my son today.' I tossed and turned in my sleep as Isaac, who was unaware of the pending sacrifice, slept like a groundhog in winter. In my half-sleep I dreamt of Isaac, bound like a lamb burning, burning, burning before the house of YHWH with all the people singing and wailing and waiting for the rains. But Isaac did not die and the skies stayed blue. Sarah bound my hands and tossed me on the fire as she stole Isaac away."

"The next day I announced that YHWH had instructed me to take my son born of Sarah to the top of Mt. Moriah and to sacrifice him. The people said, "Abraham, you must take Tobias and Aram as witnesses with you and to help make the pyre. Thinking quickly, I replied, 'The Lord our God said to me 'Abraham, go alone.'"

Now Abraham was a great prophet and no one challenged his claim. Abraham looked to his God and prayed. Then Abraham said to his son, "Gather the sheep, we must take them to the mountaintop to graze." As the sun set, Abraham, Isaac and their sheep arrived on the top of Mt. Moriah. There was no water, there was no grass, and there was no hope. Abraham said, "Isaac, we will camp here tonight." Isaac looked about and he saw nothing. The sheep, hungry and thirsty, saw there was no food or water so they lay down to die. Isaac, even though he saw there was no water or food, scrounged for some all the same. Abraham, heavy with thought and at a loss of what to do, where to go, how to avoid killing his son, took up a rock for a pillow and put his body prone, looking up for the voice of his God. Isaac saw his father lying on the bed of stone with neither food nor water, branch nor dead grass and he was puzzled. Isaac took up a rock for a pillow and lay it beside his father's stone bed and lay down onto his bed as the sun fell behind them. The sheep lay still on the mountainside. There was a great gulf of silence with neither father nor son breaking the sound of nothingness. And so the night passed. Abraham called out for his God to provide an answer, but, as he was too restless, there was no voice from his God or any other god. The sun came up and father and son could no longer ignore the other. They sat up; father with angst and a wild unkempt look that would have frightened a wolf out of his skin, and the son with searching eyes sunken deep in his head. They peered into each other's eyes for what seemed an eternity and one half. The father opened his mouth to speak, but the horror of what he had to do was too great, and his tongue froze. The son, seeing that his father could not speak, said, "Father, why did we bring our sheep to a place where there is neither food nor water?" The father again tried to speak but his lips would not move. The son said, "Father, What is the matter?" Looking away as if searching for his God, Abraham's tongue freed itself and Abraham said to his son, "Son, we are in the greatest drought of anyone's' memory. The council has pondered upon the cause of God's anger. Unsuccessful, they came to me and said, "When the gods are angry in Memphis, the pharaoh sacrifices his eldest son. When Anu is angry the Babylonian king sacrifices his eldest daughter. You must appease our God with the life of Isaac. Isaac, I don't want to sacrifice you to God. It will not help. But the people will kill us both, and Sarah and Ishmael, if I do not burn you at the pyre as sacrifice to our God. What am I to do? I have waited for a sign, but nothing."

Maddie stepped into the scene and asked, "Are you not a great prophet? Do your people believe God speaks through you? Do you think our God, who is good, would demand such a sacrifice? How could he be so angry as to say you can only have rain if you kill Isaac?"

Abraham replied, "I would rather believe there is no God than to believe he demands the life of one of his servants." Abraham got on his knees and bowed his head into the ground and said, "Oh God, my God, I need a sign, I need an omen." He bit into the dirt then lifted his chest to the sky and beat on it with both fists.

Isaac said, "Oh father, the one and only God speaks through you. Would not that god, if he spoke to you at this moment, say, 'Abraham, oh Abraham, human sacrifice is wrong. You must spare your son. Tell the people that God came to you on the summit of Moriah and said, 'I will bring rain when the omens are correct.' If you sacrifice one of my own, I will chastise all the people by silencing the rains forever.'"

Isaac picked up the prize lamb and carried it to Abraham and they knelt before their God and the sky opened and the rains came.

"Rise and Shine" "What?"

As I awoke Maddie whispered, "And so it was that Abraham ended human sacrifice among his people. The Egyptians, Babylonians and Philistines saw that it was good and in time…

"John, John, rise and shine. Breakfast is served."

March 5, 1900
Maddie,

The sun is shining. I have to plant the corn. Where are Tom and Rocco? I need them to harness Nellie. Got to get the field plowed. Are the cows milked? Where is the plow? Where is Nellie? Where am I? Maddie, I can't get out. The door is locked. Why'd you lock me in? What are you thinking? The sun is burning away. The fields are before me.

I know where I am now. The county nut house for nuts. I, John Venner, the nuttiest of them all. "Ranting and frothing in my insane crisis." I have been here forever. By myself, with you, but you are dead. Stay with me, I know you are here. I can't be alone no more. Tom comes sometimes. No one else. He tells me Frank has been here and that Ursula comes the most. I don't remember. Just Tom, I think he is the only one who came.

I don't know how I got here. When did I get here? I don't remember before. Just here, always, and there is nothing here to remember, every day the same. They wake me to feed me slop for pigs, leave me to stare at the ceiling, bring dog food for dinner, take me for a walk, "take a nap," silage for supper and once a week a bath. Nightmares with Primo. Time for slop again.

I try to remember. Our wedding, meeting you, your dad asking if I was too old, you too young, but he wanting to move and you wanting to stay -- he said fine, marry that old man if that's what you want. Helping you plant the garden, you big in the belly with our children, Tom into mischief always, yelling at Rocco, Nellie running for home, Ursula wanting to go to high school, Bessie giving more milk than any cow in Genoa, planting tobacco for the first time, the crop making more money than a year's cow milk, Lincoln getting shot, thinking I had to get out of this country – oh that was before we were married, your ground cherry pie winning the contest at the fair, talking under the moonlight before Ursula was born, you trying to get me to go to church, me finding a reason not to go, home on rainy days the kids all in school, I remember some. I see it, but so long ago, I watch from outside. I am a peeping Tom of my own life, watching from some distant place. Have I been here forever? Everything else is so far away. Has life always been here in this nut house? I don't remember coming? I can't leave. Is this all there is? All there ever was?

I have the memories, the stories. But there is no one to tell them to. Are you and Bessie and Nellie and the corn field dreams of someone else's life? Just a story somebody made up? A previous life? Another time? Only the walls are real. The locked door, the bars over its insignificant window that looks onto nothing, the unforgiving ceiling, the cold floor; they are real.

March 6, 1900

I don't know where I am. I think I been here, but I do not recognize anything. Someone brought me food. She said "Rise and shine." Later she came in and said, "Good morning, John." She knew my name. I did not know her. I asked her who she was. She laughed. Said I been flirting with her every morning for months. No way. I do not flirt.

I can play no more. I can pray no more. If only I could perish.

Maddie, I remember. It was Lucy; I am still in the nut house. I recognize it now. It is harder to hang on.

I ain't going to write that book I told you about with ten little truths. I ain't got the concentration anymore. It is getting harder and harder to write. If I could write it, how'd I get a publisher from here? And if I got a publisher, would anyone read it? I don't think America is ready for the truth, ready to become a robust nation, ready to embrace compassion. The time is not right. Maddie, Let us pray for America. Maybe, just maybe, the people will be ready to look in the mirror and see who they have become and then and then only will kindness be possible.

March 7, 1900

Maddie,

I saw you last night – in the distance – just a scarf on – flying in the wind – calling – but leaving me behind – off to shadows – turning – a smile – then poof.

I lay in bed – holding my breath "Rise & shine" she yelled – I knew I could – just stop breathing – I think I did – all went black – all went blank, I felt my soul leave. But Lucy would not leave me be; she shook me and announced in her peevish way, "Breakfast is ready. It is a lovely day. Come on John, out of bed, eat your breakfast and I will take you for a walk."

Lovely? Lovely schmovely. There is no love in this day. She went before me. There is only death, and I shall have her.

Love you more,
Giovanni

March 8

John Venner dictated the following to me on this seventh day of March in the first year of this century. -Lucy

Hi Maddie,

I don't know what day it is. I can't sit up. I can't make my hand write anymore. So I asked this pretty young nurse to write for me, Maddie. What's your name? Luke? Lucy? C. Lucy what? I knew a Lucy once. Cuter than you she was. Real cute. Maddie, I just want to join you. It is hell here. When I feel good they tie me down. When I feel bad, they take everything out of the room and I just sit here and stare at the ceiling. Please, God, let me out. Maggie, I will be with you soon. I promise.

To my children: The end is near. I know it and I long for it. I not been so good at telling you things. I want you to know I love you. I always loved you. Tom, take care of the farm. Give birth to a writer, one who can write the book I never wrote that celebrates gentle. Rocco, leave the bottle be. Mary Ann, take care of Silvie and that brood of yours. Bill, remember your mother. Jake, come home. Angie, be good to John. Ursula, I forgive you. Find my novel and finish it.

When I am gone do not cry. Be happy for me for I will join your mother. Without her I am nothing. With her ... (I waited for John to finish the sentence, but he lay motionless except for a little twitch around the right side of his lip - it could have been a smile)

March 9, 1900

Maddie, I saw a robin today.

March 10

Maddie, it is hard to breathe - to talk. I saw your

chickens on the ceiling, eggs falling into Queenie's mouth, coons up the tree, deer running wild, fox in the coop, feathers flying every which way, chickens pecking, corn fields turning sideways.

March 11, 1900

Death came in the night. He was not dressed in black but gold. He had a glowing baby face with eyes full of delight. With outstretched pudgy hand, he said, "come". I took his hand and we danced. I woke to the same damn screaming from the nutcase down the hall that wakes me every day now. Death, you are playing tricks with me. That ain't fair.

March 12, 1900

Maddie,

I am not to be denied. You will hardly know who I am or what I mean. I have stories to spare. I am the acme of things accomplished. Everything I have I bestow. You are the American Epic. I am the American Dante. "I exist as I am, that is enough." Yes, Walter, I exist as I am. Is that not enough?

[**Editor's Note:** Lucy, the nurse, added this paragraph immediately below this entry.]

March 13

After having me write this, John became silent. I went back to my other patients. Over the past weeks he has spent more and more time talking to Maddie – at first I did not know if she was real or not, then I found out Maddie was his wife and she had died not long before John came here. He

joined her during the night. His torn and tattered copy of
Leaves of Grass lay open upside down on his chest. I picked
up the book and read aloud.

> They are alive and well somewhere,
> The smallest sprout shows there is really no death,
> And if ever there was it led forward life, and does not
>   wait at the end to arrest it,
> And ceas'd the moment life appear'd.
> All goes onward and outward, nothing collapses,
> And to die is different from what any one supposed,
>   and luckier.
> Has any one supposed it lucky to be born?
> I hasten to inform him or her
> I pass death with the dying and birth with the new-
>   wash'd
> babe, and am not contain'd between my hat and boots,
> And peruse manifold objects, no two alike and every
>   one good,
>
> The earth good and the stars good, and their adjuncts
>   all good."

I thought I saw a smile on his face. Had he seen Maddie
coming just before he died or was he saying goodbye to his
beloved Walt Whitman?

-Lucy DeStefano (13 March 1900)

PS I just read through John's diary. I must give it to
Tom when he comes to bury his father.

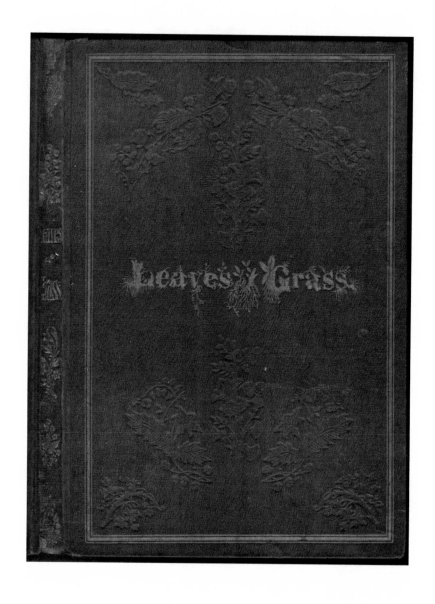

Walt Whitman

Dante

President John Quincy Adams

America's most underrated President

Homer

Thus

Spoke

the

Truth

Giovanni Vener

Cover of John's little book of truths

Tom Venner

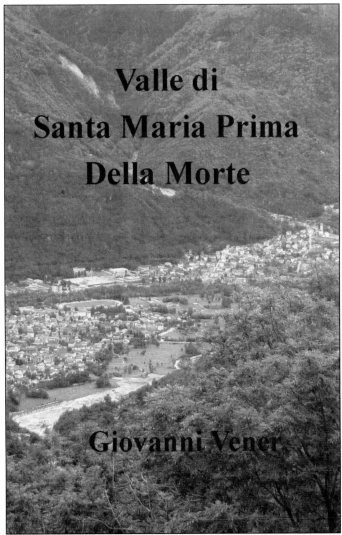

This might have been the cover for Giovanni's book about his grandmother if we had found the manuscript. As of the time of the printing of the first edition of his diary, no one has found a copy of Giovanni's book.

Genoa, Wisconsin: A Spray Drift of Empathy

For *The Story of Our Stories*, Genoa, Wisconsin, holds center stage. The coulees, bluffs, riverbed, and maybe even the pigeons called out to our immigrants to make it home; it cuddled the second generation, shaped the third, and will forever define who future generations are to become.

Genoa Village is a community in Vernon County, Wisconsin, at latitude 433436N and longitude 0911327W.

Genoa Township is located 72 through 84 miles directly north of the Wisconsin-Illinois Border and 0 to 24 miles east of the Mississippi River. If the boundary line between Iowa and Minnesota were extended across the Mississippi, it would strike about the center of section 21 of the town (in the southwest corner). Genoa is located in Wisconsin Townships 12 and 13 north. Specifically, it is comprised of Township 12, range 6 west, Sections 5-8 and 17-20; Township 12 north, range 7 west, sections 1-4, 10-16, and 21-24; and Township 13 north, range 7 west, sections 21-28 and 33-36. The total land area of approximately 22,500 acres is less than a full township of 23,040 acres.

Part I of this story appeared in Volume I, *Time to Journey Home*

Genoa: Part II
A Spray Drift of Empathy

"In 1905 Genoa had a population of 200 and about 200 families in the Township, of which about 50 were Italians. The Ticinese and the Italians had finally conquered the environment and had cleared the land they had bought as homesteaders at 5 to 10 dollars an acre. The main production consisted of: barley, corn, potatoes, clover seed, hay, tobacco and hay. Cows breeding generated milk and butter. Unexpectedly and mainly due to the climate, no grapes were grown." ["Genoa, Wisconsin and the Civil War" paper delivered by Ernesto R Milani to Italian Historical Association, 4 November 2004, p 23] "The Italians (Still considered as such) attend strictly to their farming. They are honest, peaceful and industrious." [Milani, p 24]

The first part of the twentieth century saw the building of a permanent church, a state-of-the-art two-room Catholic school, a creamery, two button factories, the Genoa Bank, and a convent to house the nuns who were recruited to teach, along with the establishment of both the Jambois and Huntington garages to take care of the needs of the growing number of automobiles. The depression led to the building of the lock and dam and the addition of electrical power, as the Roosevelt Administration created public works in order to stimulate the economy. Genoa also saw the addition of Al's Barber Shop and Clements Fishing Barge. Art Ristow, who lived across Willow Creek, delivered mail by horse and buggy, then by car, for over fifty years. For half of those years, he was the face of Genoa. He was the only other human some farmers saw during the week.

While he brought bills from the power company, he also brought cards during Christmas; from time to time, he brought a letter from the old country and on a very special occasion, a package sent directly from Sears Roebuck. He was mostly known for taking his half of the road out of the middle—but he never had an accident in all those years. Few were so welcomed by all!

He put his right finger to his nose, pushed against his nose as he thrust his finger toward you, and exclaimed, "You betcha!" when asked if his real name was G. Heileman. Every resident knew that G. Heileman Brewery Company was located in LaCrosse, Wisconsin, and most knew it was Henry Nelson's (known only as "G. Heileman") drink of choice. "G. Heileman" painted nearly every barn in Genoa Township two or three times. When called for dinner, he would stop his brush mid-stroke. "Paint will wait, but supper won't." Few paid him before the job was finished; if they did, they did not see him until he drank every cent of his wages and had time to sober up. If the paint would wait for dinner, it certainly would wait for the last dime to be spent on supporting the local brewery company.

Rarely seen, but a towering presence on the conscience of the community and a scary figure in every child's imagination, was a World War Two shell-shocked veteran who lived in a tiny shack across Willow Creek from Art Ristow's home. The tiny home, maybe 6' × 12', was built on public land just above the artesian spring that supplied water to many homes before public water became common. The vet, name unknown to many, lived there in isolation for over twenty-five years. Some claimed he lived on fish caught late at night after everyone else was asleep. He did not have a garden and rarely came out to shop for groceries. Whenever one of the school children thought they caught a glimpse of the "ghost," all were on edge for a day or two for fear "the devil" might be out and about.

Three of the Venner boys loved their booze as much as their older sisters loved their church. The youngest was a total recluse and rarely seen, except when he showed for the 10:00 AM Sunday Mass. The oldest brother was so quiet that most folks could not really tell when he was sober and when he was drunk. He collected junk and got his beer money from selling scrap iron to the smelter in LaCrosse. The middle child was a jovial drunk, stopping by any neighbor for a few hundred laughs when he was drinking. Known by all as Uncle Johnny, he always carried a few packs of grape chewing gum and handed out sticks to the kids he liked. If he decided a boy was a "no-good-for-nothing," that child never received another stick of gum no matter what he did to get back in "Uncle Johnny's" good graces.

Mid-century saw the building of a three-classroom school with an indoor gym. The old two-room school seemed fine to all, but Father Duffy [pastor from 1943 to 1952], who had won over the hearts of every parishioner, wanted a legacy, and he pushed the project forward. He talked some farmers, who rarely parted with more than a dollar at a time, into writing checks for one thousand dollars. Maybe the most welcome addition was indoor plumbing, for prior to this, students used the "two-holer." The nuns had to go back to the convent, and the eighth graders carried drinking water in every morning. Equally significant, a television sales office opened up, doing its best to speed up the use of the "radio with pictures," after the first television station in LaCrosse began to broadcast with a signal available to most residents of Genoa Township. A free trial hooked a few people, but not enough to keep the store open. Mr. Roller, the TV salesman, moved his family out of town before everyone realized how beautiful his daughters were.

Highway 35 and the railway were rerouted to bypass the town. Main street became safer and quieter, a blessing for most, but not good for the local business. Latimer's General Store had already closed and other places of business soon followed suit, including the "town institution," the Zabolio store, which struggled on until 1986.

To tell the full story of Genoa in mid-century would be to tell a tale of three towns. They were not separated by an ocean, a channel, a river, or even a stream. They were not separated by a mountain, a hill, or even a field. Nor were they separated by race, class, or sex. No, the separation was unspoken but easily as impenetrable. From the earliest settlers until mid-twentieth century, it was not so much "a community" as it was three co-existing populations sharing the same space and time—three hearts and three minds and three souls sharing the same body. The Genoa covered in our story is the town of Catholic-worshipping Italians with roots in Campodolcino and/or San Bernardo, for it is that town that reflects and defines our story of stories.

Nearly invisible to the members of this Genoa, there existed another town of non-Catholic, non-Italian citizens.

The fact that most were Scandinavian was not the defining factor; that they were not Catholic stood as the invisible but very clear barricade, keeping them as far away from the Catholic-worshipping Italians with roots in Campodolcino and/or San Bernardo as would have been true if their parents never immigrated to the USA.

The third town consisted of the Catholics whose families came from other places, including some with roots in other communities in Val San Giacomo. Even families whose roots were from Fraciscio, an outlying community of Campodolcino, lived in this faction of the town. To get an idea of their life and lifestyle, read Danielle Trussoni's memoir *Falling Through the Earth*, published in 2006. That story focuses on the life of her father who was born into a Fraciscio Catholic Genoa family. This town interacted with the Campodolcino/San Bernardo clan, but there was a clear separation of values, behavior, and socialization; even worshipping was distinct, with most of the parishioners from "Trussoni town" attending the late Mass and the Campodolcino crowd attending early Mass. Likewise, they tended to worship at different bars—Monte's Bar buzzed with activity on Sunday after Mass; another spot drew the Saturday night crowd; and a third place neither drew a crowd nor ever stood empty. Zabolio Grocery and Dry Goods Store served one town, with Latimer's store serving the other two towns. The stores were not one hundred percent segregated, but there was no question where you were most welcomed. Located at the foothill of Genoa Bluff, the Catholic Church looked out over the towns, the grocery stores, and the taverns. In the countryside, farmers tilled, planted, weeded, harvested, and milked their cows. Most citizens of our towns would have agreed with Charles Dickens's lords of the State "that things in general were settled forever."

Let's pause in the year of Our Lord one thousand nine hundred and fifty-one. Not a particularly auspicious year, but still the year we will tell about, for it was the beginning of the decade that inspired our epic—the year of the death of Peter Pedretti (who was born in Genoa before Abraham Lincoln was sworn in as the sixteenth President of the United States of America) and the year of the laying of the cornerstone for the new St. Charles School. The year 1951 was the beginning of the end of the "Genoa way of life" and the beginning of the town starting to enter mainstream America. It was the end of contentment. It was the beginning of change. It was an epoch of belief in a present that was drifting—a wellspring of hope even if they had nothing before them. It was an age of insight —it was the height of McCarthyism; it was a period of certainty— it was the beginning of doubt. It was the season of sunshine— it was a time for despair. It was the spring of expectation and it was a winter of dissatisfaction.

Each town had avoided coming into the twentieth century. True, they allowed electricity, telephones, radios, and gas engines into their lives, but their impact was minor. Life in our town was fundamentally the same in 1951 as it was when our ancestors arrived in 1854. With nine families on a party line, few used the telephone for anything but emergencies, and emergencies were so rare some phones went unused for years. Electricity powered the refrigerator, but most vegetables and fruits were still canned and meat was dried more often than frozen. The light bulb had little or no impact on bedtime or awake time; farming had to be done in daylight and the cows needed milking on schedule. Few had energy for anything but sleep after fourteen-hour work days. There was little time to sit around listening to the radio. Many listened to Paul Harvey while eating dinner—definitely a setback from pre-Paul Harvey days. Milking machines were coming into vogue by mid-century, but all knew how to milk by hand and did just that when the electric power was interrupted. Few traveled past the church or tavern of choice with their automobiles; their horses used to get them there just about as fast. The biggest change was the widespread use of tractors for plowing, cultivating, and harvesting, but this impacted only male farmers—resulting in the farmers being forced to purchase and plant a few more acres in order to support the tractor. Everyone still used their horses for many tasks such as making hay—including mowing, pulling the wagon, and providing the horse power to lift the hay into the barn by pulling the hay fork. Most still used their horses to plow the garden and to round up the cows for milking, as there were not enough tractors yet and the horses were less expensive and more efficient for many tasks.

Wood continued to be the primary source of heat, and trees were as often felled by an ax as a chain saw, which was both expensive and dangerous. Tractor-powered buzz saws helped to cut trees into sizable logs, but the wedge and sledge mauls were still the prevalent means to split the wood into usable firewood.

Genoa stayed isolated in part because the settlers had come from an area isolated by geography and attitude. It was what they knew. Equally important, they were an enclave of

Italian Catholics surrounded by Norwegian and German Protestants. Genoa was over sixty-five percent Catholic, but neighboring Vernon County was over ninety-five percent non-Catholic.

If John Venner returned in 1951, he might have been surprised by electricity, gas engines, the telephone, and radio; but he would have been completely familiar with worship practices; the celebration of holidays, weddings, and births; the games played on Sunday afternoon; the dress; the self-sufficient farmer; the political beliefs; the attitude for life; and the values of the people. With few exceptions, he would totally recognize a day in the life of a Genoa boy as detailed below.

April 12, 1951

The alarm goes off at 5:20 AM. You roll out of bed, dress, and head for the pasture to bring in the cows for the 6:00 AM milking. You and your two brothers milk the twenty-nine cows, one at a time. You wash the cows' teats, draw the milk into the milk pail, carry it to the milk house, and empty the milk into a ten-gallon milk can, which is floating in a tank cooled by spring water. You repeat this exercise until you get ten cows milked. You pour off a gallon of milk from the last cow into a pitcher that you will carry to the farm house, from which you will pour the warm milk onto your cornflakes prior to Mom putting it in the refrigerator for use that day. The clock shows 8:00 AM when you sit down for breakfast and 8:15 AM when you get back up and, depending on your age and the season, head off to school or back to the barn to clean out the gutters.

Let's say you are just shy of your twelfth birthday.

Since it is Thursday, you run out the door to jump into the back of the pick-up truck to get a ride to town along with the milk cans. Dad drives to the creamery and you help unload the cans onto the conveyer belt, which carries the cans into the cheese factory where they will be weighed before being emptied into a vat and returned to the pick-up truck. You do not wait but instead head immediately up Zabolio Hill [now called Eagle Street], walking fast so you can get in your classroom before the 8:30 AM bell. You stand, say the Allegiance to the Flag, and fall in line to walk in silence across the parking area to the church for morning Mass. Like most days, the Mass is uneventful and you instantly began to daydream. Today you daydream about discovering a way to transport milk from a cow to a house in the city without need for human labor. You see milk lines underground weaving all through the county, not unlike arteries in the body, and they are attached to the heart [the milking machine] where the blood [milk] is constantly pumped, and the family in each home can just turn on a faucet to get their supply. You invent a machine that knows when the cow steps up, hooks itself to the cow's teats, milks it, and then sends that cow on so it can get milk from the next cow. It is all automated and all free, since no humans have to be paid. Your mind takes you to a hillside pasture where everyone is free to do as they like. Some bathe in the sun, others swim in the pond, and many work together to invent better ways to make sure humans do not have to work. Some sing in a choir, others paint. There is even a clown or two to provide laughter.

Suddenly, you are startled as you are nudged to stand and walk up to take Communion. You smile, for that was a great dream. Maybe you will grow up and become famous by making it happen. Other days, you have other dreams. You remember when you were in first grade and you dreamt there were little soldiers in your body and they were waging war with each other. You thought there could be a whole world inside you with rivers flowing with some parts in peace and others at war. There were farmers planting seeds and cleaning out the gutters, bankers lending money to needy people, and doctors coming to help cure sick people. You laugh a little at yourself for imaging that. Just like there were all kinds of activities on Earth and they would be miniscule if seen from the moon, there was a whole miniature world as seen from Earth *inside you*. Your mind stops as you take Communion and you feel a little guilty for allowing your mind to wander in the presence of Jesus.

As you head back to your pew, your cheeks tighten as you recall learning about cells and germs and vitamins the previous week in science class—not that far from what you had created in your daydream a couple of years ago. Maybe ten years from now—when every house has faucets you can turn on—milk, cornflakes, and bread will flow out as easily and freely as water! You will remember you invented it in your dream today.

About once a month the Mass is a funeral Mass. You know every member of the church, and a dozen or more die every year. If burial is on a school day, you get to attend the service—in fact you have to. If the deceased is a close relative, you even get to go to the gravesite, meaning you get to skip part of the first class. On funeral days you often imagine you are in the coffin but able to hear and see what is going on.

When the priest makes up nice things about some people who you think were mean, you laugh inside thinking, "You have been such a good faker, the priest did not notice how mean you were." If your mind wanders outside the church on funeral days, it usually focuses on what it must be like to be dead. Later when you grow up, you will be dismayed at how indifferent you were to death as a twelve-year-old. Between seeing death at least weekly on the farm and monthly in the church, it was as natural to you as pretty much everything else. But now, going to a funeral is rare and painful. You go to all the weddings in the church too, but they are always on Saturday. You get out of chores to go to the Wedding Mass, but unless a relative gets married, you are right back in the fields within the hour.

School is so repetitive you do not remember much. You keep adding numbers and subtracting them. You have conjugated a thousand or more sentences. Your teachers love to make you repeat and repeat and repeat, as if no matter how many times you get it right, you must do it one more time to prove you got it right; or no matter how many times you get it wrong, if you kept repeating getting it wrong, you will somehow magically figure out how to get it right.

No amount of snow, ice, or rain can keep you from school. You remember falling down about fifty times once when the roads were pure ice. You had to crawl part of the way up Zabolio Hill. But you made it and so did almost everyone else. It would take over three feet of snow to close the school, and you do not remember that ever happening during your years at St. Charles. The only way to miss school was to come down with chicken pox, mumps, or rheumatic fever. Like everyone else, you got at least one of these once. They took you out of school for so many days you were actually happy to get back! Dad used to take your older brothers out to strip tobacco or shuck corn on Sundays, but once Father Duffy tore into him at Sunday sermon he never did that again.

You remember the year you had a nun who had just come back from a mission in China. She brought to life that old adage—there are children starving in China, so clean your plate or do whatever adults wanted you to do at the moment. At least she actually had been to China and knew firsthand that there were some starving children. The first week you were fascinated by her stories and your mind wanderings during Mass all saw you as the missionary that got all these Chinese kids out of starvation—making it impossible for any adult to ever again be able to say, "There are starving children in China so you should ...." By the third week, she apparently ran out of stories and began to repeat the same ones over and over *ad nauseam*. To this day, you flinch a little at the word "China."

The best and most useful part of school is recess. You get to play marbles, hide-and-seek, merry-go-round, or softball. When playing ball, you hope your hero in the fifth grade will pick you for his team. After they open the new school (in 1953) with a gym, you will find out what a basketball is and even play during recess when the weather is "too bad for outdoor activities."

There is always plenty of time to daydream because the teacher has four classes in her room and sometimes she has to focus on the other classes. You all study religion together, but in theory, each class is on a different level for reading and arithmetic. The times your teacher is working with the other classes is your best chance to get educated. You have time to read the encyclopedia, create more daydreams, maybe even learn what the upper class students are studying.

No loitering after school for you. Dad expects you to be home and ready to help in the fields. Some days you chop wood, and other days you pull and hoe out weeds; make hay; pick nuts, berries, or apples; mend fences; or grease machines for the next day's work. If Mom has not already prepared the chickens for tomorrow's main meal, you might get to chop the chickens' heads off and help pluck the feathers. That is more fun than working in the fields. No time to daydream, for Dad always has a chore to assign you; your goal is to get enough work done to avoid getting Dad so mad he will yell or whap you on the head. In the fall, you help butchering or make teepee-style shocks of corn by stacking the bundles of corn you just tied together. A few weeks later, you will spend many afternoons shucking the ears of corn. Mid-winter, when the weather is damp enough, you strip tobacco, separating the cigar leaves from the lesser-quality ones. Spring time, you clear the fields of rocks that the frost has brought to the surface, help plant the garden, tobacco, and corn. Sometimes you get to ride the corn planter to make sure the feeder tube does not get plugged. It is much harder planting tobacco, as each seedling has to be set in place exactly at the moment the transplanting machine spits out a pool of water into the furrow it makes, but before it closes the furrow over the roots of the plant. No time to daydream on this job!

No matter what the after-school task from fall to

spring is, you are responsible to round up the cows for milking, so you get a "break" at 5:00 PM to get the cows. This gives you time to reflect or further develop your "Mass daydream" from this morning. Supper is on the table every day at exactly 5:30 PM. Today, like nearly every other day, it consists of soup Mom calls stew—leftovers from the noon meal tossed into a stock made by boiling the chicken carcass for an hour or two in salted water and making a greasy-tasting broth that makes the stew taste like every other soup. To this day, you may still hate the taste of soup. In the summer, the stew of the day was supplemented by ears of corn, peas, beans, carrots, radishes, depending on what ripened that day in Mom's garden. In the winter, when you need some extra nourishment to confront the cold, the stew includes potatoes, and once or twice a week, warmed-up canned vegetables. You struggle to eat enough to avoid Dad or Mom trying to force you to eat more. Then it is off to milk the cows again—the same routine as morning. Milking is followed by splashing some water on your hands and arms, drying off, removing your shoes and pants, and crawling into bed by 8:30 PM. On Saturday, you get to stay up later to take your turn in the bathtub. Since you have a small septic tank, one tub of water is shared by your whole family. If you get one of the first baths, you have to go to bed earlier. If you want to stay up longer, your bath water is going to be pretty dirty. You usually choose to get the chance to stay up a little longer. When you turn fourteen, you will be allowed to stay up until 9:30 PM. You will use the extra half hour to study, read, or play Monopoly. In a few years, you will get a television set and you will watch one or two half-hour shows or the last half of an hour-long show.

Saturdays and "summer vacation" days are basically the same except, instead of going to Mass right after breakfast, you clean the manure out of the gutters. The cows stay in the stanchion for milking, and if the weather is bad, they are kept there all day and night. They are poop machines and especially like pooping when in the barn. On non-school days you take a pitch fork, attack the mixture of poop and straw, lift it into a wheelbarrow, and then wheel it outside and up the ramp where you dump it into the manure spreader. Once the barn is clean, your older brother drives the tractor and spreader out to the field where it is spread to become fertilizer so Dad can grow more corn, hay, or wheat (used mostly to feed the cows so they produce milk and make more poop). The only other difference between this day and a school day is that you go to the fields at 9:00 AM to your pre-assigned tasks after cleaning the barn—instead of at 3:00 PM after walking home from school. On most days, work in the field is more boring than difficult, but planting and harvesting days are attacked with a vengeance because you always need to complete the task before rain comes or the sun sets. There never seems to be a planting or harvesting day when there is not *two days'* work that needs to be done. If the weather is good and the prediction is sunny, Dad cuts twice as much hay as can be put up in a normal day, or he expects you to shock twice as many corn stalks. Some days, he makes your brother help plant tobacco plants until sundown, forcing you to milk not only your share of the cows but your brother's as well. The extra work caused by fear of rain coming led to many a sore muscle and evenings falling asleep while milking a cow.

If you are lucky, the Watkins man comes. He comes about four times a year and he always brings some hard candy to pass out. He has a hole in his head, and you often make up stories of how he got an indentation about the size of a quarter in his temple, which makes your brother laugh out loud. You look forward to thrashing day. Next to the Fourth of July, it is the best day of the year. The day before the thrashers come to your farm, Mom has you chop off the heads of a dozen chickens. You and your brother laugh your heads off as the chickens flop around on the ground after their beheading. Then, not so much fun, you have to pluck their feathers and gut them so they are ready for Mom to bake for the thrashers the next day. More than a dozen of your uncles, cousins, and neighbors arrive by 7:30 AM and Dad fires up the Hart-Parr and pulls the trashing machine into the field where it will do its work, separating the grain from the straw. Using a flat leather belt, he hooks the drum pulley (aka harmonic balance wheel) to the thrashing machine and engages the wheel to a cacophony of sound that will infest the air for the next ten hours. Each of the neighbors arrives with a pitchfork or a team of horses pulling a wagon. Those with a pitch fork will be thrusting it into shocks of grain, leaning back, lifting the one hundred-plus pound bundle over their heads to toss onto the wagon driven by one of the uncles. Once the wagon is loaded, the drivers turn toward the thrashing machine, pulled up next to the emptying bin, and toss the bundles in. It will shake the grain from its hull, vibrate a pan to separate the chaff from the grain, and move the grain onto a belt that conveys the grain to a bin. There it falls into an enclosed wagon to be carried to the granary, where that driver shovels it into storage. You grab a fork and head out with the loading team led by your favorite cousin. You are not strong enough to toss a full shock, even with a partner, so you toss one bundle at a time. Whenever you can get one over your head, your cousins give out a holler of approval, but mostly you have to toss them on the wagon underhanded. At 11:45 AM, half the crew walks to the house yard where a water pitcher and a wash bowl have been set up so they can splash some water onto their arms and face, thus clearing away enough chaff so they can tear into a half chicken (the men who can lift a shock by themselves get a whole chicken), a quart or two of *risot* (local dialect for risotto), some mashed potatoes and gravy, and beans freshly picked that morning by your sister. This is all washed down with a quart of Kool-Aid or milk, followed by a piece of pie—usually a quarter of the pie. You refill the pitcher as many times as needed. At 12:10 PM sharp, that crew heads back to the field to relieve the other half, who repeat the ritual described above. Once the thrashers have eaten what they want, Mom, your sisters, and your aunts who came to help bring out their plates, fill up, and head back to the kitchen where they gossip over the food for an hour or two. You get what is left over— hopefully there is some *risot* and at least one piece of pie. When you have eaten, you head back to the field until it is time to come in to milk the cows. When you get older and can toss a shock of hay with a partner, you will get to eat with the first round and can eat an entire pie if you so desire.

The only part of the week to look forward to is Sunday—in particular, Sunday afternoon. You get up the same time on Sunday and milk the cows at the same time. But after milking, you do not have breakfast, but go straight to Sunday

Mass. That means you change into your "Sunday" clothes and listen to a windy sermon telling your parents what sinners they are and/or why they should give more money to the church. Sometimes Dad or Mom gab a little after Mass and you get to hang out with a friend, but most Sundays they herd the family into the car and head home. Once in a blue moon, Mom says "Let's go to Uncle X and Aunt Y's place" and if Dad agrees, your whole family drops in unannounced for Sunday dinner. You love these days because Uncle X has lots of kids and Aunt Y makes different (therefore better) food than Mom. Even when you go right home, dinner is a banquet, usually with fried chicken, *risot*, and a slice of pie. Mom takes more time to make Sunday dinner than she does any four meals.

It is after Sunday dinner and before time to get the cows that makes Sunday so special. For five hours you have no chores or responsibilities, and you are free to do almost anything as long as it does not cost money or take you off the farm. Sometimes, if a friend has a birthday party or there is an organized ball game, you even get off the farm. You can swim in the creek, loaf, go hunting or fishing in season, play games in the woods, even invite friends over to goof off, or get up a game of Euchre. To put it in human terms, you get to be kid on Sunday afternoon.

Life for your sister is identical except she does her chores in the house instead of in the field and barn. Once you get through eighth grade, nothing will change except you will not have to go to school. Somewhere between ages sixteen and nineteen, you will take over the farm or buy your own farm and soon thereafter get married and start a family. Chances are very high your children will get to repeat your life. No doubt on April 12, 1873, your grandfather did exactly what you did today, except he had to walk to school, he milked fewer cows than you did, and his mom churned the milk into butter and sold the butter to the Zabolio Grocery and Dry Goods Store.

For the most part, Genoa has been a quiet, peace-loving town comprising people whose kindness is a model for all. Lest you think it is too good to believe, let me quote a couple of local incidents that provide the exception to help prove the rule. These stories are quoted verbatim from the *History of Vernon County,* published in 1884:

The case of State vs. Josiah Dennison for the murder of John Oliver came before Judge Bunn at the fall term of the circuit court in 1869. The facts of the case, as developed by the evidence, were as follows: There was a dance at John Briit's saloon, Genoa, formerly Bad Ax City, on Christmas Eve, 1868, which John Oliver and Dennison attended. It seems that there had been trouble between John Oliver and Warren Dennison, father of the Dennison boys. Late in the night of the dance John Oliver began to talk to James Dennison about this old grudge; but the latter told him that he did not want to have anything to say about his father's quarrels, and so the two parted without hard feeling. John Britt then got Oliver over to his house with the design of keeping him there and preventing a fracas, in the meantime Josiah Dennison had taken his partner home. After Oliver left, two friends of his began to boast that Oliver "could whip any Dennison," and offered to bet twenty-five dollars on it. This to James Dennison.

When Josiah came back, James told him what had been said, and added that the men seemed determined to bring on a fight. Josiah then went to the men who had been talking of betting, but they denied the offer of twenty-five dollars, offering a wager of five dollars instead. It appears that there was then a match made up for Josiah Dennison to fight John Oliver, the next day, it being stipulated by Dennison that he and Oliver should both be searched for weapons before the fight began. After it was settled that the two men were to fight, someone went over to Briit's and told John Oliver, who at once became enraged, put himself in fighting trim, and ran to the saloon in which the Dennisons were, calling out loudly for "that d....d Dennison who is to fight me." Those in the saloon rushed out, Josiah Dennison among the first. The two men met on the steps, Dennison saying, "Wait till 1 pull off my coat." While he was in the act of pulling off his coat the fight began, probably by Oliver striking at him. Almost as soon as they closed, Dennison called out that he was stabbed, broke loose and ran down the street, Oliver after him. Not overtaking Dennison, Oliver soon came back toward the crowd. Meeting a man in the street he asked if he was a Dennison, which was denied. Passing on he came to George Dennison and with the words, "God d d you, you are a Dennison," closed with him. George at once began to cry out to take him off that Oliver was "cutting him all to pieces." With that, Henry Dennison ran up, took hold of Oliver's shoulders, and jerked him off. Just at this instant, and while Oliver was in the attitude of striking with his knife, Josiah Dennison came up and shot him in the back of the head, about the base of the brain, causing almost instant death. The stabs inflicted upon the Dennison boys were not serious. Josiah Dennison gave himself up and upon preliminary examination was bound over to the fall term of circuit court in the sum of $1,000. A change of venue was taken to La Crosse County, where the case was finally dismissed, the killing having been so plainly justifiable.

Also the Riley boys pay dearly for stealing $92:

In the summer of 1881 Thomas and James Riley were arrested for burglary. They had entered the store building of Albert and August Zabolio, at Genoa, and stole $92. They were bound over to the circuit in the sum of $1200 each, and upon depositing the amount with the sheriff they were released upon their own recognizance. Upon gaining their freedom they both fled to some of the western territories and forfeited their bail.

Anthony Phillip Kremer was more typical of the Genoa of our story. If ever there was a parish priest whom the Catholic Church should canonize, it is the Right Reverend Kremer. He served as pastor from 1901 until his death in 1934. He oversaw the opening of the new church building on December 25, 1901, the opening of the rectory, the building of the two-room brick school house, and the establishment of a convent house for the nuns teaching in the school. He actively engaged in improving the roads in the area, leading the effort to build Highway 56 from Genoa to the county seat in Viroqua, and advocating for Highway 35 to be paved. These were material gains he brought to the town, but what he really gave was inspiration for the residents to find their best selves. Twenty-five years after his departure, parishioners would get into a discussion of this or that about the Right Reverend's words or actions, and a bystander was sure they were talking about incidents that just happened within the week. His presence remained that strong in the minds and bodies of the parishioners he so affected.

On the surface, Genoa does not look much different today than it did in Kremer's time, but its core is as changed as the bay; the distinct shoreline is replaced by a landfill to accommodate those who pass by. Most of the buildings still stand, even if used for different purposes (e.g. Zabolio Store is now an antique shop). There is a new house or two. The landscaping around the church has opened up the space and made the entrance more inviting. But neither the countryside nor the village have sustained notable change.

On the other hand, today, Father Kremer is more myth than inspiration. Few recognize the name Duffy, and the Watkins man has not made his rounds in decades. G. Heileman disappeared from his last job before ninety percent of the current residents were born. The Willow Creek shack and its "owner" are long gone. The younger residents never heard of Art Ristow. You will not meet a *Starlochi*, *Gadola*, *Paggi*, or *Francoli* coming out of the church, for "all (have) gone somewhere else. But many are still there on the steep hillside cemetery overlooking the familiar steeple of St.

Charles Borromeo Church, the Hills of Minnesota in the horizon beyond the majestic Mississippi River." [Milani, p 26]

We will end our story in mid-century, as the town began to change from what it had been, assimilating more and more into that massive wasteland known as America. Even without a Starbucks, McDonald's, or Walmart, the town can no longer maintain its distinctiveness given the proliferation of electronic devices, cheap gas, and improved roads. With the declaration of mandatory high school education, increased ease of travel, and introduction of television and Wi-Fi, the town got sucked into the current culture. It is no matter—the soul of the town lingers on in the families that chose not to leave. As mentioned in Part I of the Genoa story, "The coulee defined by the Genoa Bluff, encompassing the village of Genoa, following Highway 56 east leading to and including Mound Ridge, is not a vortex of power but a spray drift of empathy. The Genoa Drift is so calm you think nothing can happen, for the serene microbes infiltrate every nerve with germs of satisfaction into all who stand in her vapors." The Genoa Drift still binds those who return, and the stories made in these hills continue to grow in influence at unexpected times and places.

ART RISTOW

Genoa Man Carries Mail 50 Years

GENOA, Wi.s (Special) — Fifty years carrying the mail!

That's the record hung up by Art Ristow of Genoa.

Ristow started carrying the rural mail when he was 17, and serving about a year as a substitute carrier, he has continued on the job with hardly a break for half a century.

In the early days it was largely a matter of horseback or traveling on foot. Later the automobile came, but highways lagged far behind and the first roads were easier traveled by horse and buggy or even on foot.

☆ ☆ ☆

Carrying on as usual, Ristow this year is driving his 50th automobile. Averaging 15,000 miles per year on the road, Ristow in his 50 years has covered approximately 750,000 miles.

"That's a lot of mail," we suggested.

"Yep," he replied, "must be a trainload."

Monsignor A. Phillip Kremer at reception for marriage of
Paul Pedretti and Cecilia Penchi. Standing next to Kremer
is best man Victor Pedretti and right of the bride is Mary
Venner.

Sept 29, 1933

Thwarting the Deadly Trinity - the Sword, the Famine, and the Pestilence

I will send the sword, the famine, and the pestilence, among them, till they be consumed...

--Jeremiah 24:10 KJV

He who sat on it had the name Death; and Hades was following with him. Authority was given to them over a fourth of the earth, to kill with sword and with famine and with pestilence.

--Revelation 6:7-8 NASB

It is hard to imagine in the twenty-first century that there are more than a small handful of people who are enthusiasts for war, and/or starvation. Even fewer people support pestilence and death. Yet these four blights on the human race have dominated the list of humanity's top scourges since well before Jeremiah noted in the seventh century BCE that the way to pointless, premature and sometimes suicidal death was via "the sword, the famine, and the pestilence." Who can argue with the author of the "Book of Revelation" that death, pestilence, war, and famine are humanity's most damaging maladies? Yes, we all must die, but do we need to die early at the hands of war, starvation, or disease?

Let's imagine that the four banes of existence met in a

café in Rome in the spring of 1870. After gloating over their consistent and overwhelming domination over the lives of humans for millennia, their discussion leads to their future. Can they continue to rein terror over human existence?

Death speaks first, "I am perfectly safe – death is the one sure thing that will happen to all. I will reign supreme as I have since the beginning of life. In the end I will win, but I prefer not to lose too much ground along the way. I need you to do your part to keep human life short. Working together, we have kept the lifespan for humans at around thirty-one years with the days of their years limited at threescore and ten except for those who made fourscore by sheer will power. I foresee some loss of some years, unless you hold your own, for there are things in the air that spell disaster for you three. Given recent events, I predict human life expectancy will gain two to three years in the next century. I can live with that. But it will make me extremely unhappy if one of you falters in your work and we see more time added. My patience will be tried. As sure as I am that in the end I will be victorious in every case, I have no power to bring death to humans in a timely fashion. That is up to you."

War responds, "You can count on me to do my part. Yes, I know that war is the invention of mankind and all they would have to do to emasculate me would be to do nothing – that is just stay home - stop fighting. But man being man, I have reason to be confident I will deliver for you. With the on-going development of weapons of destruction, and the hardening of tribal concerns built around nationalistic states and religion, we are in for a very good century or two."

Death chimes in, "Don't be too cocky. As you said,

you are the invention of man and they could eliminate you with no effort. Certainly, recent progress in man's understanding of the world and self indicate you need to be on guard."

War boasts, "I could go to sleep for the next one hundred years and, rest assured, mankind would do my job for me." No one can make a case against War, so all eyes moved to Starvation to ask what she will do to play her role to bring suffering and early death to life on earth.

Starvation replies, "I do have much to fear. Increased harvests and the widespread introduction of vitamin rich potatoes have already weakened my power. The introduction of rail and steamboats are making it too easy to transport food from places of plenty to places of famine. Yes, I recently helped mankind uncover the wealth in the ground in order to make fuel for their use. This will make a warmer climate, thereby making more flooding and droughts, but in the end, I will need help from Disease and War to assure that I can contribute my share."

War asserts, "Count on me."

Disease brags, "Not to worry. I'm a sure bet to not only bring on early death, but enormous suffering. True, humans have made a few advancements in recent years, but there is no way they will figure out how I get them. As long as they are ignorant, I am in control. Of course, like famine, I need the help of War to spread my power. As long as War does his job, and Famine contributes, I can continue my work of spreading disease across mountains and seas and maintain my record of suffering and early death unimpeded."

Let's now imagine that a former you is sitting – in the

same year - at a local pub in Paris discussing with your fellow scientists how you can keep the four scourges of mankind at bay. No doubt everyone agrees nothing much can be done. War, death, pestilence, famine have always existed and will exist forever. But you are an idealist so you ask, "If the impact of one of these could be diminished, which would it be? All agree with little or no discussion, death is inevitable and there is nothing we can do about it. In fact, death is the by-product of the other curses. A little more discussion ensued before you agreed that pestilence is beyond the control of man. Plagues had and will continue to wipe out whole populations. Pneumonias strike at every socio-economic level. Measles respects neither race nor creed, time nor place. The enemy is too obscure to fight – all agree quickly that there is not much that humans can do to overcome pestilence.[1]

You note, "That leaves war and starvation. Certainly, we can reduce the impact of these."

The cynic among you laughs, "You are such a dreamer. Come on! From time immemorial, war, starvation, disease, and death have been the only constants besides taxes, tithes, and tolls that we can count on."

Your friend on your right, who has been studying better ways to farm, says, "We are learning better ways to keep land fertile and to increase the harvest. I know we can increase the yield of farmers – maybe even by as much as ten percent. That, by itself, would be enough to feed the world. With a little

---

[1] In 1870 a prognosticator would have been terribly optimistic to predict that the next century would see life expectancy double and a significant number of deadly diseases subjugated.

advancement in transportation and farming, we could cut starvation in half - maybe even double that. Of course, we would have to get our governments behind it and that might not be so easy."

Your friend on your left chimes in, "I agree we can and must diminish death by famine. True, we have no control over droughts and floods that can result in starvation, but in the end people starve because they do not have enough to eat, or safe water to drink. When one place suffers from drought, another place flourishes with just the right weather. We have the food to feed the world, yes?"

All have to agree. Your cynic friend asks, "But how do we get food to where it belongs before starvation sets in?" You point out the telegraph could be used to inform the world sooner of a pending tragedy, and though you personally are against the big locomotives tearing up the countryside, they could be used to transport food rapidly from a place of plenty to a place of drought. You add, "Advances in the steamship are making it possible to transport food even over the ocean in a timely fashion."

Your horticulturist friend confirms, "There can be no question that we will have the food and the ability to deliver it on time to diminish and maybe even eliminate starvation worldwide in the very near future."

Your cynic friend asks, "Yes, we may have the food - we probably will have the ability to deliver the food, but do we have the will power? In fact, do we even care?"

Your horticulture friend replies, "That may be, but I can guarantee you that new advancements in farming and gardening will assure there is enough food to feed every human in the world within a decade or two."

The physicist affirms unequivocally, "In fifty years, we will double the speed of travel; but even now we have the ability to transport food and water fast enough to prevent death by starvation in all but the most remote areas."

The historian on your right concludes, as he sips the last of his cappuccino, "I think we can agree, with some improvements in horticulture and transportation, we can reduce starvation. That is a great goal for the people of the next century. So far, we seem to agree that death is inevitable. Pestilence is beyond our control, but starvation can be reduced and, if the horticulturist is right, even eliminated. That leaves war. I must say, like death, war is as inevitable as time. I have been studying history all my life and if I have learned anything, it is that every nation worth its salt goes to war. Humanity could not advance without war. War gets a bad rap when in fact it is a big part of why we are civilized."

You stand in disbelief. You declare, "Wait a minute! Of the four historical calamities, war is the only one that is completely man-made, man-sustained, and man-perpetuated. Death is the natural result of getting older. There are unknown and probably unknowable forces behind disease. Starvation follows droughts and floods. But war – in fact - takes enormous energy, resources, and dedication from many to sustain. Mankind could end war by doing nothing. All we have to do to end war is to stay home and do nothing. Get restless? Go on vacation instead of to war – poof - war is history."

The historian replies, "You are right – to end war we have to do nothing – stay home. I like the way you think.

Think about it, my friends. To eliminate starvation will demand enormous resources, advanced transportation, and concerted cooperation of thousands. Pestilence will always be a silent killer. War, my friends, takes more effort to wage than it would take to eliminate starvation and find a cure for pestilence. Why fight? Stay home! Plow the fields! Head to the shore! I love it."

Chuckles are heard all around. You attempt to draw the discussion to a positive conclusion. "Yes, death is inevitable. There is nothing we can do to stop it, but we can postpone it by eliminating war, decreasing starvation, and monitoring pestilence. The cause of pestilence is unknown and seems beyond man's ability to control. Famine is often the result of nature, but just as often the result of war. Our farmer friend is right, even when caused by nature, we could prevent many deaths with a little ingenuity and a lot of will power. I am more optimistic than my friend. I believe our children will eliminate starvation by mid-century. But war -- now that is one hundred percent the device of mankind. Neither nature nor God can take credit. Since we invented it and we have to use enormous resources to sustain it, all we have to do is be idle. Ending war should be easier than going on vacation (you like that image). It is as easy as taking our next breath."

The more skeptical scientist replies, "You really are a romantic. We are not going to stop war by doing nothing. A Caesar, an Alexander, or a Napoleon is always waiting in the wings for the right moment to grab power and march off to conquer a little more land, if not the world. Young men looking for glory, spoils, and the opportunity to rape, will join faster than the narcissist of the day can send out a call to join."

You rejoin, "You really are a cynic. Unfortunately, you are also fundamentally right. There have been, are, and always will be those who believe their destiny is to conqueror. And yes, young males seem predisposed to fight someone else's war. But they are not chomping at the bit. Until seduced by the allure created by the warmongers, our citizens are happy to till the fields, get married, and reproduce. They have to be persuaded to fight. The would-be-conquerors use every trick in the propaganda trade to entice the young male, who may be predisposed to seek heroic opportunity, to kill and die for their ignoble enterprise."

The professor of rhetoric, silent up to now, joins the discussion. "I totally agree. The leaders who desire to add other nations to their fold study past conquerors and use the tricks of the trade to rile up the citizens to fight and/or pay for their adventures. They appeal to pride, honor, and courage. They promise great rewards (which, by the way, they never deliver) and then add guilt and fear to the mix to keep their citizens in check and their armies pumped up. The problem is the opposition is either completely silent, fails miserably to counter influence, or is put to death as traitors if they even hint at a propaganda campaign to undermine the ambitions of the "great" leader. Consequently, we have no history to study how to mount a verbal campaign to counteract the saber-rattler's propaganda machine."

The professor of agriculture speaks out, "I have known a lot of young men who clearly want no part of war, who stated they would not leave their fields and their families to go to war, but joined up as soon as the King called. Professor Rhetoric is right. The King Warrior of the day knows which buttons to push to get our young men to abandon everything they hold dear to go fight another's war. Professor Rhetoric, I hear you when you say there is no tradition of opposition. Can't you start such a tradition? We know there is a need, and you are the man with the knowledge of how to mount a successful campaign to counter the lies of the ambitious."

All eyes look to Rhetoric, "Easier said than done."

The cynic speaks, "I think it is less complicated than you make it out to be. There can be no doubt the warmongers know how to stir up the passions of their citizens especially the young males. Still there is no reason to believe that a stronger resistance campaign could not and would not gut the efforts of the war seeker. It should be easy enough to convince citizens to keep their money instead of throwing it at the King to wage war, and the young men to stay home and care for their family instead of going off to kill and to almost certainly, be killed."

All look again to Professor Rhetoric. There is a very long pause. "I have to agree, but they have a thousand years of perfecting their methods and we have none. It will take time, maybe a hundred years, to develop ways to counteract the effective tools the warriors have. I cannot go home and make up a campaign to stop war. Still, we have made a big step when we accept that it is possible and an even bigger step when we commit to make it happen. I will begin to study tonight and start developing the tools we will need within the fortnight."

You chime in, "It is possible. I am absolutely convinced that we will put an end to war and starvation before the dawning of the twenty-first century, hopefully well before that. The hand writing is on the wall. We have the understanding, the intelligence, and the tools to retire these two scourges for once and forever. We just need the will to resist the skunks who are willing to spray their venomous-fetid-conquer-ideas over normally peace-loving citizens."

In 1870, you would not have had to be a romantic to predict war and starvation would be non-existent by the end of the twentieth century. Mankind was more and more aware of the uselessness and damage of war. There was a growing movement inspired by Alfred Nobel and Baroness Bertha Sophie Felicita von Suttner to create a world government to mitigate the opportunities from which war breaks out. New advancements in agriculture and transportation accompanied with a growing realization that man's most basic right was to life would certainly lead to the end of death by starvation early in the twentieth century, if not before the end of the decade.

In 1870, I believe we would have all agreed with our friends. War could be stopped by merely not going to war, and a slight advancement in agriculture and transportation and a large increase in will power could end starvation. Putting off death and reducing the power of pestilence was impossible.

Let's transport our nineteenth century intellectuals to 2020. Let's begin by showing them the advancements in medicine that have more than doubled life expectancy and found many ways to be victorious over pestilence. No doubt they would be astonished at how the geniuses of the twentieth century pushed back the reaper and all but overwhelmed pestilence. By the time they comprehend the miracles in medicine that were accomplished, they are dying to hear how the twentieth century put war to bed forever, and to find out how many decades passed without one death by starvation anyplace in the world.

How shocked they are to find several wars in progress, and that more people died in war and genocide in the twentieth century than in all time up to 1900. How shocked they are to find that 3.5 million people die of starvation every year, and over eight hundred million citizens suffer from malnutrition. They are aghast to find out major international organizations set goals to halve the starvation rate in 1990 only to, in fact, lose ground with increases in citizens who suffer from malnutrition. Some cry and others laugh when they considered the irony of ineffectiveness of the miraculous advancements made in transportation and agriculture to remove starvation.

You have to fess up, "Yes, we have abundant food, surprisingly fast and efficient transportation systems in place, and even the will to end starvation."

Your 1870-self challenges your twenty-first century counterpart, "Why have the two scourges that could be completely eliminated not only continued to wreak havoc, but to do so on unprecedented levels? Why do humans continue to engage in war and allow starvation to reign supreme in certain parts of the world? Both could be eliminated without one thousandth of the effort that has gone into controlling disease."

You (contemporary you) have no answer. You are completely stumped, so you look to your colleagues to your right and to your left. They also look incredulous, but in a different way than your nineteenth century friends. Politician, on your right, speaks first, "You peaceniks are all so naive. Strong nations have to keep weak nations from self-destruction. If we don't contain the axis of evil countries, they will obtain and use weapons of mass destruction on civilians everywhere. There are evil people and evil nations, and they have to be contained by war or the threat of war. That's how it works. End of discussion."

You counter, "We would love to have peace, and we have been working to gain it. We believe that many of the problems that break out into war could be resolved through diplomacy, but too often our friend here undercuts discussion with his sabre rattling."

Your historian friend from the nineteenth century chimes in, "Like I said in Paris, war is inevitable. Would-be conquerors turn young bulldogs into warriors as naturally as and faster than caterpillars become butterflies. The caterpillars totally believe they will fly off in beautiful uniforms and shine in the sun of glory. The enemy – they are sure they can stop the "evil" aggressor with their own newly minted butterflies. No one acknowledges how fragile the butterfly is. Both sides get their soldiers cheap by calling on them to kill for the glory of their nation and for fear of being traitors. War is like a raging river -- it cannot be stopped and its destruction is even more inevitable. Now that weapons are as available as air, the casualties will only mount. Why are we wasting our time talking about it?"

You have to acknowledge both Mr. Politician and Mr. History have a point, but your 1870 self is not so willing to give in. "Look at the progress you have made in agriculture and transportation. You can fly surplus food to where the needy are in hours – it took us weeks, and our parents months, and still we did a better job than you are doing.

Certainly, you do not think starvation is necessary to contain the evil among you? You could knock out the effects of starvation tomorrow with minimal effort. The cost would barely be noticed by the haves, and the logistics needed pale in comparison to those needed for battle. You must agree that you should and could wipe out starvation with the blink of an eye."

"Yea, yea, every problem can be solved by government. Only in your utopia. People who work hard to get ahead ain't as willing as you think to give what they made to some lazy no-good, especially if he is from another nation," spits out of the mouth of your friend on the right.

"Even with my friend's opposition," speaks up your colleague on your left, "we could eliminate starvation. In fact, we often send plenty of food and water to prevent death. Unfortunately, the leaders of war and/or tyrants confiscate the food for their armies or themselves before it can get to the starving. Sometimes the battles prevent us from getting the food and water to those in need."

"It appears that war and war politics are the number one reason you fail to eliminate starvation," pipes up the farmer from 1870. "I believe you should all participate in eliminating starvation. After all, the cost is miniscule and the gains are humongous. Isn't it just as obvious that you cannot deliver as long as tyrants and wars flourish? You must first make war an activity of the past before you can be sure every citizen is fed. When we met back in 1870, we all agreed that it would take will and government cooperation to eliminate starvation. We also agreed that humans just had to stay home to prevent war. If no one was willing to give up their life, their livelihood, their love ones, and their future and stayed home instead of going off to kill for 'glory', the nation-builders would be emasculated. When the little Napoleons come calling, go on vacation – stay home – do not be suckered in by the slogan of the day. Let me repeat, do nothing to make war, and it will vanish as slavery has vanished. To sustain slavery, someone had to capture free men and others had to ship them to places where the law permitted other people (who were willing to hire overseers to keep slaves at work and from escaping) to buy and own other humans. Once we reduced the profit incentives in capturing, shipping, selling, and owning other humans, slavery died out. We did it against terrible odds, as slave owners assured us the world economy would collapse without slaves. It didn't. While wars were fought, and laws were passed to outlaw slavery, slavery ended when kidnappers could no longer profit from capturing and selling slaves. Transporting slaves became too difficult, and landowners finally realized it was more profitable to hire migrants than maintain slaves. If we could halt slavery upon which many relied in less than a century, then certainly you can put a stop to war which has no upsides except to a tiny number of profiteers and tyrants."

You chime in, "I have to agree. When the law of the land stopped endorsing slavery and provided appropriate penalties for continuing the practice, slavery all but disappeared. As long as slavery was legal and profitable, it flourished. As Farmer said, once there were no people financially motivated to steal, transport, and enslave other humans – socially acceptable slavery vanished."

Your twenty-first century colleague who teaches

sociology speaks up for the first time, "I see the sense in this. Any sane human would have to agree that all man has to do to end war is to stop engaging in war. Yup, ending war is as simple as doing nothing."

Your 1870 cynic friend concludes, "I think we can agree that wars are begun and sustained by avaricious profiteers with the help of glory hunting political and military leaders. Slavery was begun and sustained by avaricious land owners and debased politicians. Once the support systems that made slavery profitable were removed, the land owners lost their appetite for slavery. Can you remove the conditions that make war profitable for avaricious leaders and their financiers?"

Your new friend, the economist, notes, "Leaders do not fight their own wars any more than slave owners captured their own slaves. In the case of slaves, since they were either kidnapped or captured in war, the raw material was free. The cost of buying a slave was to cover the cost of the middle men, those who got the slave to market. If farmers gave their milk away (or had it kidnapped), the price of milk would be considerably less. War is profitable because of cheap warriors – convinced to fight not for salary but for patriotism or belief - and readily obtainable relatively cheap weapons of destruction. Why do I say relatively cheap? Because as long as there is war, the demand is great and manufacturers can mass produce – always an economic advantage."

You reply, "We can increase the cost of weapons by adding an excise tax – like the tobacco tax – make weapons so expensive that aggressors will have to hire a mercenary army and pay full price for weapons; they will soon go bankrupt.

Can we convince our young men that going on vacation is more patriotic than going to war?"

The Cynic from the twenty-first century laughs hysterically at what he believes is pure naivety among his colleagues. "Too many profit from war, and the ones who profit are in power. Nothing you say or do will ever stop war – when there are only four people left on earth, they will be engaged in a war until all are dead. That is humanity." More wild laughter.

Your cynic friend from 1870 speaks directly to twenty-first century Cynic. "You laugh at them? I laughed at my friends in 1870 – thought they were idealistic boobs. In some ways they were, but overall they were far off in their prediction that death could be put off by six to ten years in the next century. As you know, life expectancy jumped from less than forty-five years to over seventy years from 1870 to 1970. Don't be so sure war must go on. Someone can find the war gene - like biologists found the germ. Then society must commit to eradicate it. It is possible to end war and put in place systems that will prevent even one person from dying of starvation. You can and must put these two scourges onto the pages of history, as we have made slavery, human sacrifice, witch hunting, hanging, drawing and quartering, and the rack concerns of historical study featuring man's ability to be cruel.

You interrupt, "Certainly, we can all agree that war is a great contributor to starvation and that we must end war before we can hope to end starvation."

Cynic 1870 answers, "To state the obvious, something is causing war to perpetuate despite how unnatural it is, how costly it is to wage, and easy it would be to stop. The list of causes of war could go on for hours with greed, power, fame, fear, hatred, anger, and revenge toping many people's list. A cursory look at this list shows us that we have identified base emotions which define a human. We are not going to eliminate them. But do they need to lead to war? We have seen that leaders are more than willing to go to war when motivated by excess amounts of one or more of these emotions. Can we stop them, do we have the will?"

Your cynic friend from 1870 pauses, looks each person one at a time in the eye, then questions with piercing clarity, "Are we willing to emasculate warmongers to the point that it becomes impossible for someone's nation building impulse, greed, fear, hatred, desire for power, fame, and/or revenge to lead to war?" He pauses again, and then continues, "The warmongers of the world must turn citizens into cheap warriors to fight their wars, and they must arm their newly minted warriors with weapons of destruction. Can we remove the motivations that in the words of the Nazi propagandist, Hermann Wilhelm Göring, causes, 'some poor slob on a farm (to) want to risk his life in a war when the best he can get out of it is to come back to his farm in one piece?' Can we eliminate the implements of destruction that avaricious leaders need and use to create war?

Your historian friend, who fortuitously has a copy of *Nuremberg Diary* by Gustave Gilbert (Farrar, Straus & Co 1947), offers to read Herman Goering's full statement about how easy it is for avaricious leaders to recruit cheap warriors:

"Why, of course, the people don't want war," Goering shrugged. "Why would some poor slob on a farm want to risk his life in a war when the best that he can get out of it is to come back to his farm in one piece? Naturally, the common people don't want war; neither in Russia nor in England nor in America, nor for that matter in Germany. That is understood. But, after all, it is the leaders of the country who determine the policy and it is always a simple matter to drag the people along, whether it is a democracy or a fascist dictatorship or a Parliament or a Communist dictatorship." "There is one difference," I pointed out. "In a democracy the people have some say in the matter through their elected representatives, and in the United States only Congress can declare wars."

"Oh, that is all well and good, but, voice or no voice, the people can always be brought to the bidding of the leaders. That is easy. All you have to do is tell them they are being attacked and denounce the pacifists for lack of patriotism and exposing the country to danger. It works the same way in any country."

Your socialist friend's veins are popping, "Call it patriotism, nationalism, chauvinism, xenophobia, or tribalism. It boils down to the cry that will rally the troops even when they are not in danger or exposing themselves to danger. Hitler bought the Germans to do his "bidding" -- not because they were in danger, but because he 'denounced the peacemakers for their lack of patriotism.'"

Your historian friend chimes in, "Patriotism only exists in nation states. Karen Armstrong makes a very strong case in *Fields of Blood* that war did not exist until the Sumerian nation-state, the prototype nation-state, came into existence. Before that, scrimmages between tribes were more "raids" than wars. If my tribe needed or wanted your tribe's goods and/or women, we raided your tribe. We had no intention or interest in dominating you or wiping you out. That would be self-defeating – who would we raid next time we needed goods or fresh genes to keep our bloodline from over-inbreeding? To build a nation-state, the epic hero of Sumer, Gilgamesh, had to conquer and subdue neighboring tribes and turn them into willing and cheap warriors. These warriors would in turn capture more tribes and then to defend the new country from 'being attacked' by other aggressive tribes fearful of being subdued by Sumer. From the beginning, war was to a nation-state what sugar is to candy, milk to a baby, consumer to a corporation, and carrion to a vulture. It is not possible for the latter to exist without the manifestation of the former."

The 1870 cynic agrees, "Raids no longer served primarily to provide food in time of need and/or tribal survival by avoiding inbreeding. For Gilgamesh and all the Gilgameshes since, intra-tribal conflict was about nation-building, legacy building, and/or protecting your nation-state against the insatiable appetites of other nation-states' leaders. Leaders soon learned what Goering articulated - if you want poor farmers (who have a whole lot to lose and nothing to gain by going to war) to fight for your nation building instinct, accuse them of being cowards and unpatriotic if they dare utter a peep of resistance. If that does not work, hang and quarter them for being traitors. Thus, war was invented and sustained."

Your socialist friend points out, "Early leaders also found it advantageous to add the lure of religion to the call for patriotism. Early and present-day warmongers not only call on the citizens (usually reduced to subjects) to war by appealing to their 'patriotism' but they also use ambitious religious leaders to claim that the gods demand service. If you die in war for your mortal master, your immortal master(s) will reward you in death. While pagan gods could inspire warriors, belief in a single god (therefore the one and only) created martyrs - individuals more than willing to happily die for their beliefs and convictions, to become suicide "bombers" by recklessly endangering their own lives in order to infiltrate the enemy. A martyr, by definition, is willing to die (aka commit suicide) - willing to unquestionably die - for those leaders who dared to claim some connection to a higher authority. Death in battle for nation building – suicide by war - is no different than suicide by cop, except in suicide by war there is a promise of eternal glory while suicide by cop merely means an end of personal agony."

Your historian friend adds, "For millennia, ambitious leaders used the gods to eke out victories or justify losses. Then an ambitious member of a Roman triumvirate bested the use of gods to create killer soldiers. Constantine, who was losing the ongoing battle between Rome and Byzantium, observed how Christians were absolutely devoted and willing to sacrifice even their lives for their cause. He weaponized their fanaticism in order to strengthen his army by declaring Christianity the state religion. He successfully recruited Christian citizens as warriors to help him defeat his fellow emperors, Maxentius and Licinius, in a series of civil wars. He thus became the sole ruler of both west and east by 324 AD. Inspired by Constantine's insight, every manifest destiny nation since has capitalized on the use of monotheism to recruit martyrs for the 'holy' cause – to increase their boundaries and/or influence."

You think out loud, "Isn't it obvious that the first step to eliminate war is to dismantle the nation-state structure and to reduce or eliminate the influence monotheism has to subjugate the populace to fight cheap?"

Your socialist friend pounds on the table. "Eliminate patriotism and religion, and avaricious leaders will have to hire mercenaries at top dollar, as there will be no "free" army of patriots, and the cost will be too great for the potential gains."

The cynic cautions, "That may not be true as long as our malevolent leaders have access to cheap weapons of destruction. A mercenary army armed with massive amounts of cheap and easily available and replaceable weapons of destruction could still engage in war. So, let's eliminate weapons of destruction. Imagine a world with no nations, no suicide promoting (aka martyrdom worshipping) religion, and no weapons of destruction. Would war still be possible? Imagine an ambitious leader who cannot appeal to patriotism or monotheism to raise funds and/or to volunteer soldiers willing to fight cheap, and has no weapons of destruction at his disposal. At best he could hire some mercenaries to rein terror with brute force, but the possible damage would be limited, and the resources necessary to maintain his aggression would soon run out."

Our 1870 farmer-philosopher joins in, "By now you must be thinking – sure if we could eliminate these things, there would be no war – wouldn't it be easier to just eliminate war? Citizens all over the world worship their nation, their one and only God, and their guns. Even people living in substandard conditions are still willing to fight and die for their leader – North Korea, The Islamic State of Iraq and al-Sham, and Russia are just three examples. You could easily make the case that we cannot overcome the power of accusing the citizen of being unpatriotic and un-monotheistic -- especially the power of the call to be able to die a martyr and receive untold Benes in the afterlife. Please stay with me as I explore the possibility."

The socialist interrupts, "I agree that mankind has a solid record of being able to eradicate socially accepted, government sponsored, religiously demanded destructive manmade behavior. Evil systems once held sacred and fully supported and encouraged by state and religion have been eradicated or reduced to illegal underground activity."

The farmer continues, "I have already pointed out that our ancestors eliminated government supported slavery. Slavery existed long before war. It was thought by one civilization after another that slavery was as necessary as oxygen to sustain life on earth. Not only did nobles and warriors deem slavery a necessity, but many slaves would have agreed. Slavery too was human made and human supported at great sacrifice for all. Low and behold, human civilization did not crumble with the abolishment of slavery. Nor did the world end when societies abandoned human sacrifice to the gods. Or animal sacrifice. Yet for untold millennia, the layman, the intellectuals, the shaman, the rulers had no doubt that the gods would wreak havoc over the universe if not offered up a young virgin now and then, and lambs on an on-going basis."

The rhetorician adds, "We no longer seek out witches

under the auspices of protecting our citizenry from the evil influences of the devil. Public hangings are no longer used to deter thieves. Disembowelment, dismemberment, impalement, hanging and quartering, the rack, breaking wheels, burnings, and crucifixion are no longer used to punish infidels, traitors, or others considered threatening to the state or church. These outrages were the direct results of public policy sustained by widespread belief that these actions were required for the safety and growth of mankind. Most believed the very survival of humanity depended on their continuation. Yet, as humanity evolved, each was proven of no value and eliminated. In our time what is more destructive than war – certainly, it is as manmade and man sustained as human sacrifice, witch hunting, medieval torture, slavery, and public hangings."

Your historian friend offers context. "The first step to eradicate past horrors usually rested in the hands of those thinkers, scientists, and artists who envisioned a world without these policies and behaviors and clearly saw they were neither necessary, productive, nor natural behaviors."

Enthused, you jump in, "We need an artist or a prophet, an Abraham (one could make the case he led the charge to eliminate human sacrifice), a Magna Carta - step one to the demise of divine rights - a James Madison, the primary author and promoter of the Bill of Rights of citizens, or a William Wilberforce who led the charge that was the beginning of the end of transporting slaves to lead us out of a quagmire and onto a higher plane.

Your poet neighbor, who joined the group late proffers, "Let's listen to John Lennon's 'Imagine there is no

Heaven.'" The poet recites the song.

The historian continues, in a near whisper, "Are you willing to imagine a world with no countries, no tribes, and no ethnic infections around which you can rally the troops for the purpose of killing others? If there are no countries, acquisitive leaders cannot bring the people to do their bidding, in Hermann Wilhelm Göring's words, by telling 'them they are being attacked and denounce the peacemakers for lack of patriotism and exposing the country to danger.'"

The 1870 cynic leans in, "Are you willing to imagine a world with no heaven, no hell, no religion, a world where no acquisitive ruler (in Seneca the Younger's words) can use religion 'regarded by rulers as useful' to rally the layman to war because 'religion is regarded by the common people as true'? (Edward Gibbon, *The History of the Decline and Fall of the Roman Empire*, Vol. I, Ch. II) There will be no citizens turned warriors killing randomly - in an effort to thwart those who are not of our god, our tribe, our non-existent ephemeral race, our pretend ethnicity - of their most basic right as humans – the right to life."

Your 2020 cynic colleague challenges all at the table, "I will deviate from Lennon's trinity of 'can you imagine' and ask you if you can imagine a world with no nations, no religion, and no weapons of destruction - a world void of the opportunity for acquisitive rulers to wage war or even a lone gunman to take multiple lives without the effort you would need to pull a few weeds from your garden? I repeat, can you imagine a world with no nations, no religion, and no guns? If you can, we can create that world - a world with no war, no starvation, no racism, no sexism, no classism."

Our 1870 cynic tries to conclude the discussion. "Is it just a crazy dream? Can we eliminate independent nations as we know them? Can we overcome the role of monotheism to support and stimulate war and prejudice? Can we eliminate weapons of destruction, the requisite tools of warmongers? Please note that nations, religion, and weapons of destruction, like war, are completely man-made and only exist by Herculean efforts to maintain them!"

Your friend on your left wonders, "Maybe it is within our power to eliminate war and poverty, and along with them racism, sexism, and classism, since these are all activities or policies perpetrated solely by man; but I think most would agree, 'no way, it cannot be done, war is as inevitable as death, poverty is an inescapable hazard of market forces, and humans are inherently ranked.'"

Reader, you may be thinking, "These beliefs are so ingrained and so much a part of everyday deeds, only a clown dare even mention a world without them."

Allow me to join the conversation and summarize our imaginary colleague's points. When famine and pestilence threatened whole populations, the need to placate gods and raid other tribes' store houses seemed and maybe was necessary to survive. Faced with sure death for all, offering a few prize virgins up to powerful gods seemed to make more than a little sense. When the long held morality codes of the medieval ages seemed to be crumbling, burning a few witches to scare parishioners back into what was believed God-ordained behavior seemed a small sacrifice to get the necessary results. Nation building came about when agriculture developed enough to make conquering other tribes more profitable than merely raiding them.

Eventually, the evidence proved that the gods were not listening; human sacrifices were futile, "witches" had no influence, and the "revered" behavior being protected by law was man-made and destructive, supported by leaders especially suspect to corruption. They created systemic chaos, including declaring war that was solely designed to protect, endorse, and enhance the privileges of the suppressor class.

For the past millennium, it has been obvious that the loss of goods and life in war far outweighed the gain of conquering your neighbor. Since World War Two, it is clear that it is no longer possible to conquer your neighbor or to create a better regime through revolution. There can never again be a "winner" of a war. There will only be losers and those that lose even more. No one won the Korean War, the Vietnam War, the wars over Afghanistan, or the Iraqi wars. No one will be a winner when the Syrian revolt dies out. The evidence is irrefutable -- we just have to listen to it. War no longer has any upside, if it ever did.

Each of the listed socially acceptable, government sanctioned, ritualized by religion human behavioral systems that in time became unthinkable, emerged because of a strongly felt need man had when they became ways of life. Each continued long after it was obvious they had no use, and in fact were destructive. Eventually, however, each was eradicated. The need for war to sustain nations has long passed; the time to end war forever is now.

We will not eliminate war by saying it no longer exists, nor by proving you can only lose. This would not happen even by creating a worldwide propaganda campaign ten times greater and more effective than the warmongers can mount. It will not be possible to eradicate war until we degrade all nations. Avaricious leaders of nations will take their countries to war in a romantic notion that they can win and conqueror, as long as they have discounted soldiers to fight, using easily obtained weapons of destruction. Citizens will fight to avoid being considered a traitor to their state or an infidel to their religion. Weapons of destruction in the hands of citizen-soldiers can provide cowardly rulers the incentive to game war as they sit on the sidelines, believing they have little to lose (and in their ego-fantasies, much to gain).

Our new friends have demonstrated, beyond a reasonable doubt, that war is under-pinned by the powerful trinity of nation-state sustained by religious conviction, with unlimited access to weapons of destruction. We must supersede the sovereignty of nations while simultaneously eradicating all weapons of destruction and creating the milieu for corporate religion to fade away.

As demonstrated, the record clearly proves that humanity can replace deeply held long practiced destructive behavior. Were any of these policies or behaviors any more or less inherent to human nature than war or poverty? I think not. In fact, quite the contrary is true. All were believed at the time they flourished as ways to better man's position. I cannot imagine there are more than a tiny number of people in the world today that think war, poverty, and starvation promote the welfare of humanity. These pestilences will be easier to eradicate – not easy, but easier than the destructive behaviors our ancestors banned, as they genuinely believed their very existence depended on human sacrifice, slavery, and witch burnings.

To repeat one final time, the triune sustaining war well beyond its era of usefulness is tribalism/nationalism (nation-states), monotheism (fundamentalism), and possession of weapons of destruction. The task to eliminate them will be complicated of course, because war returns the favor by sustaining and nurturing nationalism, monotheism, and the manufacture and use of weapons of destruction. But the vicious cycle can and must be broken. It is inevitable. This world cannot continue to tolerate violent behavior of human on human. Come, imagine a world free of war, free of starvation, free of racism, sexism, and classism, and free of violence. Join us now - let the world live as one. What do you have to lose, my friend?

Book VII

Diary of Giovanni Vener

Appendices

Appendix A

Mary Madeline Starlochi

Meet Giovanni Venner's wife, Mary Madeline Starlochi, and her ancestors. Mary Madeline was born in Campodolcino and immigrated, with her parents, to Bad Ax, Wisconsin as a child. Her parents were also born in Campodolcino and baptized at St. John the Baptist Church. All of their known ancestors were born, lived and died in Val San Giacomo; a small valley located about eighty-five miles north of Milano. Our story traces Mary Madeline's linage back 11 generations to her great-great-great-great-great-great-great-great grandfather Guglielmo Chiaverini who was born in 1566 of whom we know little except he fathered Sebastiano Chiaverini in 1601 and that he died on 26th day of April 1649. The Starlochi family was well established and was almost certainly among the first to settle in the valley.

Note about naming

Our Italian ancestors had well-established customs in the naming of their children. In Val San Giacomo, a couples' first son was traditionally named after the paternal grandfather. The second son was named after the maternal grandfather, the first daughter was named after the paternal grandmother, and the second daughter was named after the maternal grandmother. If a couple had more than four children, they may have chosen names of aunts, uncles, cousins or close friends for the succeeding children.

Should a child die in infancy, a couple often named their next baby with the same name to preserve the naming patterns and/or to carry on the spirit of the deceased child.

Ahnentafel Chart - Mary Madeline Starlochi

This is the account of all the known ancestors - as of publication - of Mary Madeline Starlochi who was born on 18 Apr 1849 in Campodolcino, Sondrio, Lombardy, Italy. Her ancestors are presented in the strict numbering order created and first used by Michaël Eytzinger in 1590. This table includes the full name of each ancestor as well as the dates and places of birth, marriage, and death if known.

First Generation

1. **Mary Madeline STARLOCHI** was born on 18 Apr 1849 in Campodolcino, Sondrio, Italy. She died on 10 May 1899 in Genoa, Wisconsin. She was buried in St. Charles Cemetery, Genoa, Wisconsin. She immigrated to the USA in 1854 with her parents and her younger sister Maria.

Mary married **John Baptist "Giovanni" VENNER** son of Giovanni Primo VENER and Margherita DELLA MORTE about 1867 in Genoa, Wisconsin. John was born on 13 Mar 1829 in Campodolcino, Sondrio, Italy. Even though her husband was 20 years her senior, he outlived her. John died on 13 Mar 1900 in Viroqua, Vernon, Wisconsin. He was buried in St. Charles Cemetery, Genoa, Wisconsin.

Mary Madeline gave birth to ten children including Bartholomew "Tom" Venner, the father of Agnes whose story is told in Book IX. Seven of her children lived to maturity.

Second Generation

2. **Bartholomew "Bartolomeo" STARLOCHI** was born on 24 Sep 1825 in Campodolcino, Sondrio, Italy. He died on 5 Aug 1900 in St. Paul, Ramsey, Minnesota. He was buried on 7 Aug 1900 in Sacred Heart, Aberdeen, Brown, South Dakota. He married Marianna ZABOLIO on 5 Mar 1847 in Santuario di Gallivaggio, Gallivaggio, Sondrio, Italy.

3. **Marianna ZABOLIO** was born on 17 Dec 1823 in Campodolcino, Sondrio, Italy. She died on 6 Feb 1905 in Aberdeen, Brown, South Dakota. She was buried on 7 Feb 1905 in Sacred Heart, Aberdeen, Brown, South Dakota.

Mariana gave birth to ten children, seven lived to maturity.

Mary Ann Zabolio (1823 – 1905)
Bartholomew Starlochi (1825-1900)

Santuario di Gallivaggio,
Gallivaggio, Sondrio, Italy.
Church where Bartholomew and Mary Ann wed.

Obituary of Bart Starlochi
as published by "The Aberdeen Daily News"
Dated Aug. 6, 1900.

A telegram received yesterday brought the information that B. Starlochi died in St. Paul Sunday morning, Aug. 5, 1900 at 10 o'clock. The message came as a shock to his family and friends, as it was supposed that he was getting along well. A week before he had gone to St Paul, accompanied by his son-in-law John Briedenbach, and Father O'Hare to have a surgical operation performed for the relief of a malady for which he had suffered intensely for about five years. The surgeons performed the operation on Wednesday morning and the results appeared to be most satisfactory for a couple of days, since which, until the announcement of his death no information had been received.

B. Starlochi was born in Como, Italy in 1825, and he came to this country about 45 years ago, his wife following a year or two later. He located at Galena, Ill. and after a year relocated to Genoa, Wis. where he conducted a mercantile business and managed farms until he came to Spink County SD about 16 years ago. He devoted his time here to the supervision of farming interests he acquired. He possessed a fine business ability and was very successful being worth a large amount of money at the time of his death.

His aged wife survives him and five out of the ten children born to them are living, all being daughters. Three of these ladies live in Aberdeen, namely, Mrs. John Briedenbach, Mrs. George Lupi, and Mrs. Tillie Shook, the others being Mrs. Rosa Zabolio, of Genoa, WI., and Mrs. A. Ott of Edgerley, ND.

The remains will be brought to Aberdeen this evening or tomorrow morning and the funeral will take place from Sacred Heart of Jesus Church on Tuesday forenoon at 10 o'clock.

Obituary of Marianna Zaboglio Starlochi published by "The Aberdeen Daily News" Dated February 6, 1905

Mrs. Mary Ann Starlochi (Marianna Zaboglio) passed away this morning at 6:30 o'clock at the residence of her daughter, Mrs. Adolph Ott, after suffering from a long attack of pneumonia. She was one of the oldest residents of the city, being at the time of her death over 81 years of age.

The funeral will be held tomorrow afternoon at the Church of the Sacred Heart at 2:30 O'clock and will be conducted by Rev. Father Dermody, pastor of the church.

The deceased was born in Northern Italy December 17, 1823. She married Bartholomew Starlochi while they lived in Italy, in 1847. They settled at Galena, Ill. where they resided for about a year and a half. They then removed to Genoa, Wis. where they stayed until 1884, when they removed to the extreme southern part of Brown County. About ten years ago they removed to this city. Her husband died about four years ago.

To Mr. and Mrs. Starlochi ten children were born, six daughters and four sons. All of the sons died before reaching maturity, and one daughter Mrs. John Venner, died some time ago at Genoa, Wis. leaving a family of seven children. The names of the children who survive their mother are Mrs. John Briedenbach of this city, Mrs. George Lupi of Minneapolis, Mrs.

Albert Zabolio of Genoa, Wis., and Mrs. Adolph Ott and Mrs. Edward Shook, both of this city.

Mrs. Starlochi was a woman of much property and was well known by her many acts of charity among the needy of the city. She delighted in using her means to relieve suffering, and she won a host of friends among those to whom she administered. She was one of the foremost in the support of the Sacred Heart Church, of which she had been a member ever since she removed to Aberdeen. Everyone who knew her was drawn to her by her generous and sympathetic qualities. She will be greatly missed by the community in which she lived. She will be buried tomorrow afternoon in the Catholic Cemetery.

The following was published in the Aberdeen Daily News on Feb. 8, 1905 with some modifications.

The funeral of Mrs. Mary Starlochi was held yesterday afternoon at the Church of the Sacred Heart, the Rev. Father Dermody, pastor of the church officiating. The funeral was largely attended by the many friends and relatives of the deceased, all of her five living daughters being present. They are Mrs. John Briedenbach, Mrs. Adolph Ott, and Mrs. Edward Shook of this city, Mrs. George Lupi of Minneapolis and Mrs. Albert Zabolio of Genoa, Wis. The interment was in the Catholic Cemetery.

The author of an Aberdeen's Sacred Heart Parish history published some years later wrote "An Italian gentleman, Mr. Starlochi is given credit for supervising a fund drive to purchase a bell for the new Sacred Heart Church. This bell was placed in the first church's frame structure. It was later moved to the new brick church, still later to the present church. It is possibly the only item from the original church that is still in use today".

Third Generation

4. **Agostino Giuseppe STERLOCCHI** was born on 18 Jul 1779 in Campodolcino, Sondrio, Italy. He died on 6 Sep 1850 in Italy. He married Maddalena GIANOLI on 29 Jun 1812 in Italy.

5. **Maddalena GIANOLI** was born on 7 Oct 1781 in Italy. She died on 16 Aug 1846 in Italy. Maddalena gave birth to 7 children, five lived to maturity.

6. **Francesco Giuseppe ZABOGLIO** was born on 25 May 1801 in Sondrio, Italy. He died on 27 Feb 1836 in Italy. He married Maria Teresa Domenica. P. BUZZETTI on 27 Feb 1821.

7. **Maria Teresa Domenica. P. BUZZETTI** was born on 20 May 1797 in Vho, Sondrio, Italy. She died on 10 Sep 1862 in Genoa, Vernon, Wisconsin. Maria Teresa Domenica gave birth to seven children; five lived to maturity.

Francesco Zaboglio was the son of Agostino Zaboglio. Agostino was active in Campodolcino, Sondrio, Italy. We have found records dating the Zaboglio families' activities in the area back to 15 Century in the Campodolcino area. Francesco operated a stagecoach that delivered mail from Genoa, Italy through the Alps to Geneva, Switzerland. He was killed in 1836, by an avalanche, when his youngest son John B Zabolio was 3 months old. He left a widow with five surviving children, all who were to later come to America and all settled in Genoa for at least a generation before leaving for other areas in the US. As the name was Americanized the "g" was eliminated to spell their name as Zabolio.

Fourth Generation

8. **Bartolomeo STERLOCCHI** was born on 11 Jun 1742 in Campodolcino, Sondrio, Italy. He died on 11 Nov 1813 in Italy. He married Domenica GHELFI on 25 Feb 1767 in Italy.

9. **Domenica GHELFI** was born on 26 Apr 1735 in Italy. She died on 28 Sep 1781 in Italy. Dominica gave birth to fourteen children; it is believed that ten lived to maturity.

10. **Gabriele GIANOLI** was born on 4 Sep 1748. He died on 29 Mar 1820. He married Marta Elisabetta BRUNI on 10 May 1773.

11. **Marta Elisabetta BRUNI** was born on 23 Feb 1756. She died on 14 Jan 1790.

12. **Agostino ZABOGLIO** was born on 9 Sep 1776 in Italy. He died on 30 Mar 1803 in Italy. He married Lucrezia GADOLA on 19 Feb 1800 in Italy.

13. **Lucrezia GADOLA** was born on 9 Apr 1778 in Italy. She died on 15 Jun 1803 in Italy. Lucrezia gave birth to at least

two children

14. **Giovanni Battista BUZZETTI IV** was born on 2 Feb 1763 in Vho, Sondrio, Italy. He died on 6 Jun 1820 in Mese, Sondrio, Italy. He married Marianna CERLETTI on 18 Aug 1791.

15. **Marianna CERLETTI** was born on 12 Nov 1767 in San Bernardo, Sondrio, Italy. She died on 5 Nov 1833 in Vho, Sondrio, Italy. Marianna gave birth to ten children.

Fifth Generation

16. **Guglielmo STERLOCCHI** was born in 1705 in Italy. He died before 1784 in Italy. He married Maria Caterina BUZZETTI on 4 Oct 1727 in Campodolcino, Sondrio, Italy.

17. **Maria Caterina BUZZETTI** was born on 19 Oct 1702. She died on 26 Sep 1754. Maria Caterina gave birth to at least four children.

18. **G Battista GHELFI** was born on 15 Jan 1708. He died on 30 Jan 1775. He married Anna Maria FUSTELLA on 6 Mar 1728.

19. **Anna Maria FUSTELLA** was born on 3 Feb 1704. She died on 3 Jan 1793. Anna Maria had at least two children.

20. **Giovanni Pietro GIANOLI** was born on 10 Apr 1721. He died in 1799. He married Maddalena M GHELFI on 7 Apr 1747.

21. **Maddalena M GHELFI** was born on 6 Apr 1727. She died on 19 Mar 1757.

22. **Gabriele BRUNI** was born on 19 Jun 1731. He died on 5 Oct 1758. He married M Maddalena CURTI on 21 Apr 1755.

23. **M Maddalena CURTI** was born on 7 Apr 1736. She died on 19 Apr 1780.

24. **Francesco Antonio ZABOGLIO** was born on 2 Mar 1754 in Italy. He died on 24 Aug 1830 in Italy. He married Annamaria P GUANELLA on 1 Jun 1774.

25. **Annamaria P GUANELLA** was born on 4 Mar 1744 in Italy. She died on 5 Aug 1793 in Italy.

26. **Giuseppe GADOLA** was born in 1739. He died on 16 Apr 1806. He married Orsola DELLA MORTE on 10 Mar 1763.

27. **Orsola DELLA MORTE** was born on 17 Mar 1744. She died on 3 Jan 1802.

28. **Giovanni Battista BUZZETTI III** was born on 22 May 1730 in Vho, Sondrio, Italy. He married Domenica ADAMOSSI on 20 Aug 1758.

29. **Domenica ADAMOSSI** was born on 6 Aug 1728 in Lirone, Sondrio, Italy.

30. **Lorenzo Giuseppe CERLETTI** was born on 8 Dec

1725 in San Bernardo. He died on 17 Jan 1775. He married Teresa FALCINELLA on 17 Sep 1759 in San Bernardo, Sondrio, Italy.

31. **Teresa FALCINELLA** was born on 6 Oct 1737 in San Bernardo. She died on 16 Aug 1807.

Sixth Generation

32. **Antonio STERLOCCHI** was born in 1679. He died on 15 Apr 1751. He married Anna Marie ROMITOLI.

33. **Anna Marie ROMITOLI** was born in 1679.

34. **Giovanni Battista BUZZETTI** was born on 21 Feb 1666. He died on 3 Jul 1737. He married Maria ZABOGLIO on 29 Sep 1697.

35. **Maria ZABOGLIO** was born on 2 Sep 1669. She died on 16 Nov 1737.

36. **Giovanni Pietro GHELFI** was born on 11 Feb 1662. He died on 8 Dec 1725. He married Guglielma GIANUCCHI.

37. **Guglielma GIANUCCHI** was born in 1673. She died on 14 Dec 1732.

38. **Guglielmo FUSTELLA** was born in 1652. He died on 13 Jan 1712. He married Angela GIANOTTI.

39. **Angela GIANOTTI** was born on 29 Apr 1667 in Gallivaggio, Italy.

40. **Gabriele GIANOLI** was born in 1694. He married Maria SCARAMELLA on 26 Sep 1715.

41. **Maria SCARAMELLA** was born in 1696. She died on 13 Dec 1765.

42. **Francesco GHELFI** was born in 1687. He died on 30 Mar 1747. He married Antonia MANINI on 18 Jun 1713.

43. **Antonia MANINI** was born in 1692. She died on 20 Apr 1745.

44. **Gabriele BRUNI** was born on 20 Nov 1698. He died on 22 Jan 1735. He married Maria TINI on 27 May 1727.

45. **Maria TINI** was born on 27 Jan 1705. She died on 11 Jun 1782.

46. **Lorenzo CURTI** was born in 1688. He died on 18 Jun 1749. He married Marta Orsola CURTI on 8 Jul 1713.

47. **Marta Orsola CURTI** was born in 1690. She died on 27 Dec 1741.

48. **Agostino Gabriele ZABOGLIO** was born on 3 Nov 1719 in Campodolcino, Sondrio, Italy. He died on 23 Nov 1791 in Italy. He married M Caterina GHELFI on 17 Aug 1741 in Italy.

49. **M Caterina GHELFI** was born on 25 Dec 1715 in Italy. She died on 25 Oct 1776 in Italy.

50. **Pietro GUANELLA** was born on 9 Sep 1704. He died on 5 Jun 1775. He married Marta GIANOTTI on 9 Feb 1733.

51. **Marta GIANOTTI** was born on 7 Mar 1709. She died on 12 May 1778.

52. **Giovanni Battista GADOLA** was born in 1691. He married Margherita GIANOTTI on 26 Apr 1720.

53. **Margherita GIANOTTI** was born on 1 Sep 1697 in Lirone. She died on 21 Aug 1751.

54. **Giovanni DELLA MORTE** was born on 20 Nov 1709. He died on 8 May 1770. He married Lucrezia SCARAMELLA on 24 Sep 1736.

55. **Lucrezia SCARAMELLA** was born on 10 Feb 1713. She died on 15 Nov 1785.

56. **Giovanni Battista BUZZETTI II** was born on 10 Dec 1706 in Vho, Sondrio, Italy. He died on 3 Aug 1781. He married Maria GIANOTTI on 18 Nov 1728.

57. **Maria GIANOTTI** was born in 1708 in Lirone, Italy. She died on 8 Mar 1774.

58. **Guglielmo ADAMOSSI** was born in Lirone, Sondrio, Italy. He married M Elisabetta GIANOTTI on 9 Oct 1709.

59. **M Elisabetta GIANOTTI** was born on 22 Feb 1688. She died on 21 Mar 1738.

60. **Stefano CERLETTI** was born in 1684 in San Bernardo. He died on 23 Apr 1742. He married Anna ZERLETTI.

61. **Anna ZERLETTI** was born in 1689 in San Bernardo. She died on 24 Mar 1759.

62. **Giovanni FALCINELLA** died on 2 May 1712. He married Domenica AGOSTI.

63. **Domenica AGOSTI**

Seventh Generation

64. **Guglielmo STERLOCCHI** was born in 1648 in Campodolcino, Sondrio, Italy. He died on 1 Sep 1719. He married Maria Caterina POLETTA on 23 Jul 1669 in Campodolcino, Sondrio, Italy.

65. **Maria Caterina POLETTA** was born in 1648 in Portarezza, Campodolcino, Sondrio, Italy. She died on 18 Aug 1720.

66. **Antonio ROMITOLI**

68. **Bartolomeo BUZZETTI** was born in 1625. He married Maria SCARAMELLA on 31 Aug 1646.

69. **Maria SCARAMELLA** was born in 1628. She died on 18 Mar 1683.

70. **G Battista ZABOGLIO** was born in 1634. He died on 16 Dec 1679. He married Agnese SCARAMELLA on 9 Sep 1656.

71. **Agnese SCARAMELLA** was born in 1631. She died on 13 Apr 1694.

72. **Giovanni Battista GHELFI** was born in 1625. He died on 23 Jul 1705. He married Caterina MANINI on 1 Feb 1659.

73. **Caterina MANINI** was born in 1630.

74. **Giovanni GIANUCCHI** was born in 1636. He married Maria BONOLI on 9 May 1661.

75. **Maria BONOLI** was born in 1641. She died on 26 Aug 1697.

76. **Giovanni Benedetto FUSTELLA** was born in 1609. He died on 12 May 1704. He married Domenica DELLA MORTE on 12 May 1642.

77. **Domenica DELLA MORTE** was born in 1622. She died on 28 Sep 1690.

78. **Giovanni Antonio GIANOTTI** married Giovannina GIANOTTI.

79. **Giovannina GIANOTTI** was born in 1645. She died on 4 Jan 1720.

80. **Gabriele GIANOLI** was born in 1655. He died on 8 Mar 1720. He married Lucia TOMELLA on 27 Jul 1677.

81. **Lucia TOMELLA** was born in 1651. She died on 27 Apr 1728.

82. **Pietro SCARAMELLA**

84. **Guglielmo GHELFI** was born in 1649. He died on 13 Mar 1699. He married Caterina TINI on 9 Jan 1673.

85. **Caterina TINI** was born in 1657. She died on 5 Nov 1736.

86. **Gaudenzio MANINI** was born on 7 Sep 1662. He died on 23 Aug 1720. He married Caterina BARINCELLI on 18 Feb 1686.

87. **Caterina BARINCELLI** was born in 1661. She died on 8 Aug 1702.

88. **Giovanni Battista BRUNI** was born on 21 Mar 1666. He died on 13 Jan 1714. He married Maria TINI.

89. **Maria TINI** was born in 1670. She died on 1 Nov 1727.

90. **Pietro TINI** was born in 1679. He died on 31 Jul 1714. He married G Maria CAMAGGIO.

91. **G Maria CAMAGGIO** was born in 1686. She died on 13 May 1725.

92. **Giovanni Battista CURTI**

94. **Giovanni Antono CURTI** was born in 1652. He died on 14 Dec 1692. He married Elisabetta GIANOTTI on 13 Sep 1688.

95. **Elisabetta GIANOTTI** was born on 18 Aug 1666. She died on 4 Apr 1757.

96. **Agostino ZABOGLIO** was born in 1671. He died on 28 May 1745. He married Maria GIANOLI on 27 Nov 1698.

97. **Maria GIANOLI** was born in 1680. She died on 23 Aug 1753.

98. **Francesco GHELFI** was born in 1687. He died on 30 Mar 1747. He married Antonia MANINI on 18 Jun 1713.

99. **Antonia MANINI** was born in 1692. She died on 20 Apr 1745.

100. **Giovanni Pietro GUANELLA** was born on 24 Jan 1665. He died on 30 Aug 1727. He married Domenica TINI on 29 Dec 1692.

101. **Domenica TINI** was born on 15 Feb 1664. She died on 25 May 1742.

102. **Bartolomeo GIANOTTI** was born in 1669. He died on 1 Feb 1741. He married Maria MANINI on 18 Oct 1695.

103. **Maria MANINI** was born in 1672. She died on 6 May 1744.

104. **G Battista GADOLA** was born in 1652. He married Maria VANOSSI on 6 May 1677.

105. **Maria VANOSSI** was born in 1660. She died on 29 Jan 1698.

106. **Guglielmo GIANOTTI** was born in 1655 in Lirone, Sondrio, Italy. He died on 7 Apr 1711. He married Caterina LOMBARDINI.

107. **Caterina LOMBARDINI** was born in 1656. She died on 26 Aug 1715.

108. **Giovanni DELLA MORTE** was born in 1662. He died on 3 Dec 1731. He married Maria BARILANI on 21 Sep 1689.

109. **Maria BARILANI** was born on 20 Jun 1669. She died on 19 Mar 1737.

110. **Giovanni Donato SCARAMELLA** was born in 1694. He died on 3 Aug 1762. He married Orsola RIZZI.

111. **Orsola RIZZI** was born in 1694.

112. **Giovanni Battista BUZZETTI I** was born on 1 Jul 1677 in Cimaganda, Sondrio, Italy. He married Lucrezia GIAMBELLI.

113. **Lucrezia GIAMBELLI** was born in 1688. She died on 23 Feb 1723.

114. **Guglielmo GIANOTTI**

116. **Antonio ADAMOSSI**

118. **Guglielmo GIANOTTI** married Guglielma GIANOTTI.

119. **Guglielma GIANOTTI**

120. **Stefano CERLETTI** married Anna Maria GADOLA.

121. **Anna Maria GADOLA** was born in 1651. She died on 27 Jan 1727.

122. **Giorgio ZERLETTI** was born in 1649 in San Bernardo. He died on 4 Aug 1705. He married Anna PEDRONI.

123. **Anna PEDRONI** was born in 1666 in Gallivaggio. She died on 21 Mar 1726.

124. **Giovanni FALCINELLA**

126. **Cristoforo AGOSTI**

Eighth Generation

128. **Antonio STERLOCCHI** was born in 1618. He died on 1 Sep 1691.

130. **Francesco POLETTA**

136. **Guglielmo BUZZETTI** was born in 1599. He died on 29 Dec 1659.

138. **Giovanni Battista SCARAMELLA**

140. **Guglielmo ZABOGLIO** was born in 1584. He died on 3 Dec 1651. He married Dominica.

141. **Dominica** was born in 1593. She died in 1653.

142. **Guglielmo SCARAMELLA**

144. **Pietro GHELFI**

146. **Gaudenzio MANINI** was born in 1600. He died on 10 Dec 1683.

148. **Giovanni Battista GIANUCCHI**

150. **Giovanni Battista BONOLI**

152. **Benedetto FUSTELLA**

154. **Rocco DELLA MORTE**

156. **Guglielmo GIANOTTI** was born in Cimaganda.

158. **Guglielmo GIANOTTI**

160. **Pietro GIANOLI**

162. **Giovanni Pietro TOMELLA**

168. **Giovanni Pietro GHELFI** was born in 1598. He died on 18 Sep 1661.

170. **Giovanni Pietro TINI** was born in 1622. He died on 1 May 1672. He married Maria ZABOGLIO on 3 Jul 1656.

171. **Maria ZABOGLIO**

172. **Giovanni Pietro MANINI** was born in 1635. He died on 17 Feb 1677. He married Maria CHIAVERINI on 22 Jul 1659.

173. **Maria CHIAVERINI** was born in 1636. She died on 29 Apr 1702.

174. **Giovanni Giacomo BARINCELLI** was born in 1626. He died on 12 Aug 1677. He married Caterina ROSSOTTI.

175. **Caterina ROSSOTTI** was born in 1628. She died on 25 Aug 1691.

176. **Giovanni BRUNI** .Giovanni married Maria

FANETTI.

177. **Maria FANETTI** was born in 1627. She died on 4 Oct 1700.

178. **Gabriele TINI**

180. **Pietro TINI** married Maria GIANOLI.

181. **Maria GIANOLI**

182. **Benedetto CAMAGGIO** was born in 1642. He died on 14 Dec 1726. He married Marta PEDRONI.

183. **Marta PEDRONI** was born in 1650. She died on 17 Mar 1734.

188. **Giacomo CURTI** was born in 1600 in Starleggia, Sondrio, Italy. He died on 20 Jan 1676. He married Marta CURTI on 29 May 1642.

189. **Marta CURTI** was born in 1619.

190. **Francesco GIANOTTI** was born in 1632. He died on 24 Jun 1702. He married Elisabetta MACOLINO on 11 Jun 1657.

191. **Elisabetta MACOLINO** was born in 1636.

192. **G Battista ZABOGLIO** was born in 1634. He died on 16 Dec 1679. He married Agnese SCARAMELLA on 9 Sep 1656.

193. **Agnese SCARAMELLA** was born in 1631. She died on 13 Apr 1694.

194. **Gabriele GIANOLI** was born in 1655. He died on 8 Mar 1720. He married Lucia TOMELLA on 27 Jul 1677.

195. **Lucia TOMELLA** was born in 1651. She died on 27 Apr 1728.

196. **Guglielmo GHELFI** was born in 1649. He died on 13 Mar 1699. He married Caterina TINI on 9 Jan 1673.

197. **Caterina TINI** was born in 1657. She died on 5 Nov 1736.

198. **Gaudenzio MANINI** was born on 7 Sep 1662. He died on 23 Aug 1720. He married Caterina BARINCELLI on 18 Feb 1686.

199. **Caterina BARINCELLI** was born in 1661. She died on 8 Aug 1702.

200. **Guglielmo GUANELLA** was born in 1644. He died on 4 Jul 1683. He married Annamaria TINI on 6 Aug 1662.

201. **Annamaria TINI** was born in 1643. She died on 8 Jun 1673.

202. **Gabriele TINI** was born in 1639. He married Margherita GHELFI on 14 May 1663.

203. **Margherita GHELFI** was born in 1637 in Portarezza. She died on 18 Nov 1671.

204. **Francesco GIANOTTI** was born in 1632. He died on 24 Jun 1702. He married Elisabetta MACOLINO on 11 Jun 1657.

205. **Elisabetta MACOLINO** was born in 1636.

206. **Giovanni Pietro MANINI** was born in 1635. He died on 17 Feb 1677. He married Maria CHIAVERINI on 22 Jul 1659.

207. **Maria CHIAVERINI** was born in 1636. She died on 29 Apr 1702.

208. **Agostino GADOLA**

210. **Guglielmo VANOSSI** was born in 1615. He married Lucia PELAPANE on 19 Jun 1644.

211. **Lucia PELAPANE**

212. **Guglielmo GIANOTTI**

214. **Giacoma Antonio LOMBARDINI** was born in 1619 in Fontana. He married Anna VANOSSI on 20 Jun 1645.

215. **Anna VANOSSI** was born in Prestone, Sondrio, Italy.

216. **Guglielmo DELLA MORTE**

218. **Giovanni Battista BARILANI** married Domenica

FUSTELLA.

219. **Domenica FUSTELLA** was born in 1623. She died on 11 Jan 1698.

220. **Antonio SCARAMELLA**

222. **Guglielmo RIZZI**

224. **Giovanni BUZZETTI** was born in Vho, Sondrio, Italy. He married Domenica GIAMBELLI.

225. **Domenica GIAMBELLI**

226. **Francesco GIAMBELLI** married Giovanni BUZZETTI.

227. **Giovanni BUZZETTI**

236. **Giacomo GIANOTTI**

238. **Guglielmo GIANOTTI**

242. **Giovanni GADOLA**

244. **Lorenzo ZERLETTI**

246. **Guglielmo PEDRONI**

Ninth Generation

256. **Giovanni Battista STERLOCCHI** died before 1641.

280. **Bartolomeo ZABOGLIO**

342. **Guglielmo ZABOGLIO**

344. **Gaudenzio MANINI** was born in 1600. He died on 10 Dec 1683.

346. **Sebastiano CHIAVERINI** was born in 1601. He died on 4 Feb 1664.

348. **Pietro BARINCELLI**

354. **Andrea FANETTI** died on 17 Feb 1674.

364. **Giovanni Giacomo CAMAGGIO** was born in 1596. He died on 15 Apr 1659.

366. **Guglielmo PEDRONI** married Maria DELLA MORTE on 7 May 1649.

367. **Maria DELLA MORTE**

376. **CURTI Agostino**

380. **Giovanni Battista GIANOTTI**

382. **Bartolomeo MACOLINO**

384. **Guglielmo ZABOGLIO** was born in 1584. He died on 3 Dec 1651. He married Dominica.

385. **Dominica** was born in 1593. She died in 1653.

386. **Guglielmo SCARAMELLA**

388. **Pietro GIANOLI**

390. **Giovanni Pietro TOMELLA**

392. **Giovanni Pietro GHELFI** was born in 1598. He died on 18 Sep 1661.

394. **Giovanni Pietro TINI** was born in 1622. He died on 1 May 1672. He married Maria ZABOGLIO on 3 Jul 1656.

395. **Maria ZABOGLIO**

396. **Giovanni Pietro MANINI** was born in 1635. He died on 17 Feb 1677. He married Maria CHIAVERINI on 22 Jul 1659.

397. **Maria CHIAVERINI** was born in 1636. She died on 29 Apr 1702.

398. **Giovanni Giacomo BARINCELLI** was born in 1626. He died on 12 Aug 1677. He married Caterina ROSSOTTI.

399. **Caterina ROSSOTTI** was born in 1628. She died on 25 Aug 1691.

400. **Giovanni Battista GUANELLA** was born in 1616. He died on 5 Jul 1671. He married Maria PARACCHINI on 3 Jun 1643.

401. **Maria PARACCHINI** was born in 1625.

402. **Giovanni Pietro TINI** was born in 1605. He died on 10 Feb 1671. He married Domenica VANONI.

403. **Domenica VANONI** was born in 1610. She died on 16 Jun 1673.

404. **Pietro TINI** was born in 1608. He died on 6 May 1678.

406. **Guglielmo GHELFI** was born in 1602. He married Maria.

407. **Maria**

408. **Giovanni Battista GIANOTTI**

410. **Bartolomeo MACOLINO**

412. **Gaudenzio MANINI** was born in 1600. He died on 10 Dec 1683.

414. **Sebastiano CHIAVERINI** was born in 1601. He died on 4 Feb 1664.

420. **Antonio VANOSSI**

422. **Antonio PELAPANE**

430. **Simone VANOSSI**

436. **Francesco BARILANI**

438. **Benedetto FUSTELLA**

448. **Giacoma BUZZETTI**

450. **Bernardo GIAMBELLI** was born in Vho, Sondrio, Italy.

452. **Antonio GIAMBELLI**

454. **Antonio BUZZETTI**

488. **Laurenti ZERLETTI**

Tenth Generation

512. **Donato Battista STERLOCCHI**

692. **Guglielmo CHIAVERINI** was born in 1566. He died on 26 Apr 1649.

708. **Giovanni Battista FANETTI**

732. **Bernardo PEDRONI**

734. **Giovanni DELLA MORTE**

768. **Bartolomeo ZABOGLIO**

790. **Guglielmo ZABOGLIO**

792. **Gaudenzio MANINI** was born in 1600. He died on 10 Dec 1683.

794. **Sebastiano CHIAVERINI** was born in 1601. He died on 4 Feb 1664.

796. **Pietro BARINCELLI**

802. **Pietro PARACCHINI**

804. **Giovanni TINI**

806. **Giovanni VANONI**

808. **Giovanni TINI**

828. **Guglielmo CHIAVERINI** was born in 1566. He died on 26 Apr 1649.

896. **Antonio BUZZETTI** was born in 1570.

Eleventh Generation

1588. **Guglielmo CHIAVERINI** was born in 1566. He died on 26 Apr 1649.

Appendix B

Genoa Postcards

Circa 1876

Circa 1880

Circa 1895

Circa 1903

Circa 1908

1912

The photograph below is dated 1912. Most noticeable is the fact that the rail tracks now cross what used to be the Genoa Bay, cutting it off from the Mississippi River except for the bridge shown on the upper left side of photo. August Zabolio's prominent home is front center. His store dominates Main Street and the new brick bank is open for business. Left of the bank you see the corner of Starlochi's original home.

Circa 1925

Circa 1929

Circa 1942

Circa 1957

Circa 1976

2010
Photo by Michela Fanetti

Appendix C

Pedigree Chart

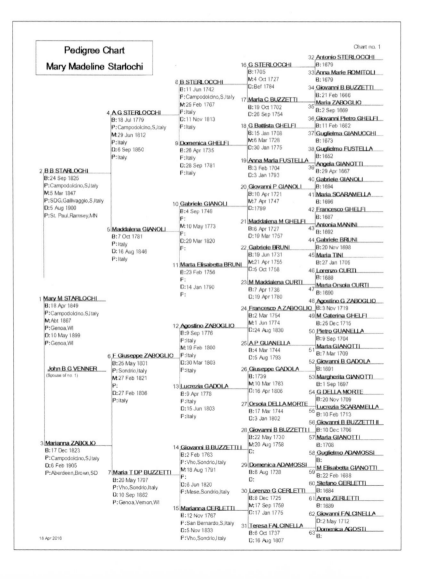

Pedigree Chart

Mary Madeline Starlochi

Chart no. 1

Appendix D
Primary Documents John Venner Family

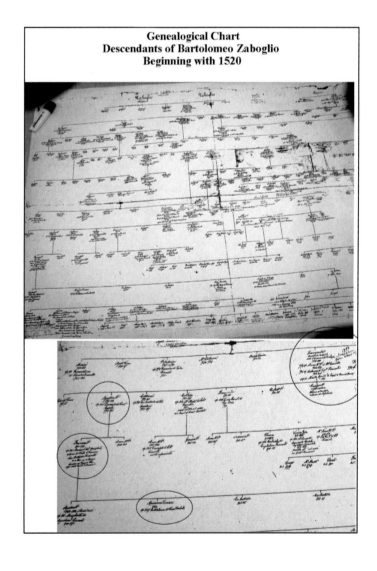

Genealogical Chart
Descendants of Bartolomeo Zaboglio
Beginning with 1520

Membership Chart Val San Giacomo Council
Francesco, Egidio Andrea and Placido Vener
Year Ca 1820

BARTHOLOMEW ⅃ MARY ANN ZABOLIO
STARLOCKI
Married 1850 - United states

Mr. & Mrs. Bartholomew and Mary Ann Starlocki

It is unclear why this photo is dated 1850. They were married in Italy on 5 March 1847 and did not immigrate until 1854. It is likely this photograph was taken at their wedding or on an annivsersary after they immigrated.

Land Grant Patent to John Venar (Venner) dated 5 August 1885. These two 40s are still owned by one of Giovanni's great grandchildren.

Final Certification of Naturalization
Bartholomew Starlocki
30 June 1890

4732   FINAL CERTIFICATE OF NATURALIZATION.

UNITED STATES OF AMERICA.

COUNTY COURT.   STATE OF SOUTH

Spink COUNTY.   DAKOTA.

BE IT REMEMBERED, That on the *30th* day of *June*
in the year of our Lord one thousand eight hundred and ninety, personally appeared
before the Honorable *Isaac Howe*
Judge of the County Court of *Spink* County, in the State aforesaid,
Bartholomew Starlocki an alien born, above the age
of twenty-one years, and applied in open Court to be admitted to become a naturalized citizen of the UNITED
STATES OF AMERICA, pursuant to the several acts of Congress heretofore passed on that subject. And the
said *Bartholomew Starlocki* having thereupon produced to the Court
record testimony showing that he had heretofore reported himself and filed his declaration of his intention to
become a citizen of the United States, according to the provisions of said several acts of Congress, and the Court
being satisfied as well from the oath of the said *Bartholomew Starlocki*
as from the testimony of *Joseph Breidenbach*
and *Fred Fischbach* who are known to be citizens of the United States,
that the said *Bartholomew Starlocki* has resided within the limits and
under the jurisdiction of the United States, for at least five years last past, and at least one year
last past within the State of South Dakota, and that during the whole of that time he has behaved himself
as a man of good moral character, attached to the principles contained in the Constitution of the United
States, and well disposed to the good order, well being and happiness of the same, and two years and upwards
having elapsed since the said *Bartholomew Starlocki*
reported himself and filed his declaration of intention as aforesaid:
IT WAS ORDERED, that the said *Bartholomew Starlocki*
be permitted to take the oath to support the Constitution of the United States, and the usual oath whereby he
renounced all allegiance and fidelity to every foreign Prince, Potentate, State or Sovereignty whatever, and
more particularly to *The King of Italy*
whereof he was heretofore a subject, which said oath having been administered to the said
Bartholomew Starlocki by the Clerk of said Court, it is ordered
by the Court that the said *Bartholomew Starlocki* be admitted to all
and singular the rights, privileges and immunities of a naturalized citizen of the United States, and that
the same be certified by the Clerk of this Court, under the seal of said Court, which is done accordingly.

By the Court, *Isaac Howe* Judge.
Attest: *C. A. Dabre* Clerk.
B. R. Smith Deputy
TESTIMONY That the foregoing is a true copy of the proceedings taken from the
record of the proceedings of the Court aforesaid, I subscribe my name
hereunto and affix the Seal of the County Court, this *30th*
day of *June* in the year of our Lord one thousand
eight hundred and ninety.

C. A. Dabre Clerk.
By *B. R. Smith* Deputy.

Certificate of Death
John Venner
March 13, 1900

VERNON COUNTY } SS

I, VERA J. NELSON, REGISTER OF DEEDS in and for said County and State, do hereby certify that the attached copy of DEATH is filed in Volume 3 Page 38 and is a true and correct copy on file in this office. IN WITNESS WHEREOF, I have hereunto set my hand and seal at Viroqua, Wisconsin, this 14th day of OCTOBER , 1997.

VERA J. NELSON, REGISTER OF DEEDS

38   Registration of

No. 25

1. Full name of deceased	John P. Venner
2. Maiden name, (if wife or widow)	
3. Color	White.
4. Sex	Male.
5. Race (s)	Italian
6. Occupation of deceased	Farmer.
7. Age (years, months, and days)	70
8. Name of father	—
9. Birthplace of father	—
10. Name of mother	—
11. Birthplace of mother	—
12. Birthplace of deceased	Italy.
13. Name of wife of deceased	
14. Name of husband of deceased	
15. Date of birth of deceased	1830. maybe
16. Condition (single, married, or widowed)	Married.
17. Date of death	Mch. 13. 1900.
18. Residence at time of death	Vernon Co. Asylum for chronic insane
19. Cause of death { Primary / Secondary }	Insanity / Exhaustion of chronic dementia
20. Place of death	Vernon Co. asylum for chronic ins
21. Duration of disease	Four years
22. Was the deceased ever a soldier or sailor in the service of the United States?	
23. Place of burial	Genoa, Vernon Co. Wis
24. Name of undertaker or other person conducting burial	
25. Date of certificate	Mch 13, 1900.
26. No. burial permit	
27. Date of burial permit	Mch. 13, 1900.
28. Other important facts not related	

Obituary
Bartholomew Starlocki
August 5, 1900

⊃IARLOCKI, Bartholomew

Starlocki, Bartholomew

DEATH OF B. STARLOCKI

Death Ends His Sufferings In St. Paul Sunday Forenoon

A telegram received yesterday brought the information that B. Starlocki died in St. Paul Sunday morning at 10 o'clock. The message came with a shock to his family and friends, as it was supposed that he was getting along well. A week before he had gone to St. Paul, accompanied by his son-in-law, John Breidenbach, and Rev. Fr. O'Hora, to have a surgical operation performed for the relief of a malady from which he had suffered intensely for about five years. The surgeons performed the operation on Wednesday morning and the result appeared to be most satisfactory for a couple of days, since which, until the announcement of his death, no information had been received.

Mr. Starlocki was born at Como, Italy, in 1825, and came to this country about forty-five years ago, his wife following a year or two later. He located at Galena, Ill., and after a year removed to Genoa, Wis., where he conducted a mercantile business and managed farms until he came to Brown county about sixteen years ago. He devoted his time here to the supervision of farming interests he

acquired. He possessed a fine business ability and was very successful, being worth a large amount of money at the time of his death.

His aged wife survives him and five out of ten children born to them are living, all being daughters. Three of these ladies live in Aberdeen, namely, Mrs. John Breidenbach, Mrs. George Lupie and Mrs. Tillie Shook, the others being Mrs. Rosa Zebolia of Genoa, Wis., and Mrs. A. Ott of Edgeley, N. D.

The remains will be brought to Aberdeen this evening or tomorrow morning and the funeral will take place from Sacred Heart of Jesus church on Tuesday forenoon at 10 o'clock.

Certificate of Marriage
Bartholomew "Tom" Venner
Mary Nichelatti
29 April 1902

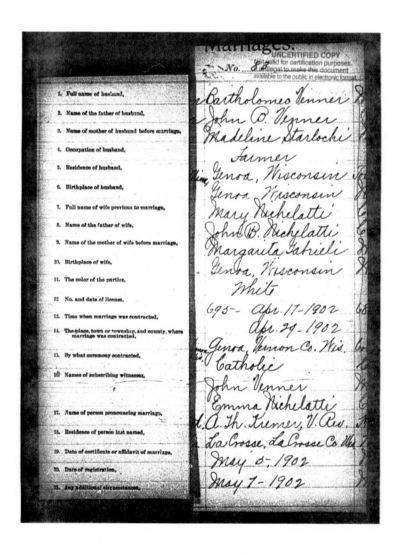

Obituary
Mary Starlocki
6 February 1905

MRS. MARY STARLOCKI EXPIRES

Passed Away This Morning After a Long Illness of Pneumonia

Mrs. Mary Starlocki passed away this morning at 6:30 o'clock at the residence of her daughter, Mrs. Adolph Ott, after suffering from a long attack of pneumonia. She was one of the oldest residents of the city, being at the time of her death over 81 years of age. The funeral will be held tomorrow afternoon at the Church of the Sacred Heart at 2:30 o'clock and will be conducted by Rev. Father Dermody, pastor of the church.

The deceased was born in Northern Italy December 17, 1823. Her maiden name was Mary Ann Zabolio. She was married to Bartholomew Starlocki shortly after coming to this country in 1850. They settled at Galena, Ill., where they resided about a year and a half. They then removed to Genoa, Wis., where they stayed until 1884, when they removed to the extreme southern part of Brown county. About ten years ago they removed to this city. Her husband died about four years ago.

To Mr. and Mrs. Starlocki ten children were born, six daughters and four sons. All of the sons died before reaching maturity, and one daughter, Mrs. Venner, died some time ago at Genoa, Wis., leaving a family of seven children. The names of the children who survive their mother are Mrs. John Breidenbach of this city, Mrs. George Lupie of Minneapolis, Mrs. Albert Zabolio of Genoa, Wis., and Mrs. Adolph Ott and Mrs. Edward Shook, both of this city.

Mrs. Starlocki was a woman of much property and was well known by her many acts of charity among the needy of the city. She delighted in using her means to relieve suffering, and she won a host of friends among those to whom she administered. She was one of the foremost in the support of the Sacred Heart church, of which she had been a member ever since she removed to Aberdeen. Every one who knew her was drawn to her by her generous and sympathetic qualities. She will be greatly missed by the community in which she lived. She will be buried tomorrow afternoon in the Catholic cemetery.

Mary Starlocki Funeral
Press Coverage
7 February 1905

The funeral of Mrs. Mary Starlocki was held yesterday afternoon at the Church of the Sacred Heart, Rev. Father Dermody, pastor of the church, officiating. The funeral was largely attended by the many friends and relatives of the deceased, all of her five daughters being present. They are Mrs. John Breidenbach, Mrs. Adolph Ott and Mrs. Edward Shook of this city, Mrs. George Lupie of Minneapolis and Mrs. Albert Zabolio of Genoa, Wis. The interment was in the Catholic cemetery.

13 Feb. 1905 p.4
8 Feb. 1905 p.8 ADN

Certificate of Death
Margaret Nickelatti
23 July 1926

Form 209—9-12-25—60M

STATE OF WISCONSIN
Department of Health—Bureau of Vital Statistics

UNCERTIFIED
NOT VALID FOR
IDENTIFICATION PURPOSES

ORIGINAL CERTIFICATE OF DEATH

1 PLACE OF DEATH

County _Monroe_

Township _Genoa_

or Village

or City

(If death occurred in a hospital or institution give its NAME instead of street and number.)

Registered No. _3_

FULL NAME _Margaret Nickelatti_

(a) Residence. No. _Geno. Wis._ St. Ward.

(Usual place of abode) (If nonresident give city or town and state)

Length of residence in city or town where death occurred yrs. mos. ds. How long in U. S., if of foreign birth? yrs. mos. ds.

PERSONAL AND STATISTICAL PARTICULARS

3 SEX _Fem_ **4 COLOR OR RACE** _White_ **5 SINGLE, MARRIED, WIDOWED OR DIVORCED** (Write the word) _Married_

5a If married, widowed, or divorced HUSBAND of (or) WIFE of _John Nickelatti_

6 DATE OF BIRTH (month, day and year) _Feb 16 1855_

7 AGE Years _71_ Months _5_ Days _6_ If LESS than 1 day, hrs. or min.

8 OCCUPATION
(a) Trade, profession, or particular kind of work _Housewife_
(b) General nature of industry, business, or establishment in which employed or (employer)

9 BIRTH PLACE (State or country) _Tyrol, Italy_

10 NAME OF FATHER _John Gabriel_

11 BIRTHPLACE OF FATHER (State or country) _Italy_

12 MAIDEN NAME OF MOTHER _Not Known_

13 BIRTHPLACE OF MOTHER (State or country)

14 THE ABOVE IS TRUE TO THE BEST OF MY KNOWLEDGE
(Informant) _John Nickelatti_
(Address) _Genoa Wis_

15
Filed _July 26_, 19 26 _G H Loofboro_ Registrar
Paid Up Sub-Registrar

MEDICAL CERTIFICATE OF DEATH

16 DATE OF DEATH _July 23 1926_ (Month) (Day) (Year)

17 I HEREBY CERTIFY, That I attended deceased from _July 15_, 19 26, to _July 23_, 19 26, that I last saw her alive on _July 22_, 19 26, and that death occurred on the date stated above, at _5_ m

The CAUSE OF DEATH* was as follows: _Cardio vascular disease_

(Duration) yrs. mos. ds.

Contributory (SECONDARY) _Foster_

(Duration) yrs. mos. ds.

18 Where was disease contracted if not at place of death? _No_

Did an operation precede death? _No_ Date of

Was there an autopsy? _no_

What test confirmed diagnosis?

(Signed) _M. D._

July 24, 19 26 (Address) _La Crosse Wis_

* State the disease causing death, or in deaths from VIOLENT CAUSES state (1) means and nature of injury, and (2) whether accidental, suicidal or homicidal. (See reverse side for additional space.)

19 PLACE OF BURIAL, CREMATION OR REMOVAL _Genoa Wis_ **DATE OF BURIAL** _7 28 6_ 19

20 UNDERTAKER _A J Mills_ **ADDRESS** _La Crosse_

Certificate of Death
John M Nickelatti
17 August 1932

Certificate of Death
Bartholomew "Tom" Venner
16 April 1946

Form No. 206-8-46-75M
Copy Certificate of DEATH

WISCONSIN STATE BOARD OF HEALTH
Bureau of Vital Statistics

106

Local Registrar's No. _____

Please Cooperate. Use black ink to improve a photostatic copy of this record for legal purposes.

1. PLACE OF DEATH:
   (a) County __Vernon__
   (b) Township _____ or — City or Village __Genoa__
   (c) Name of hospital or institution __Residence__

2. USUAL RESIDENCE OF DECEASED:
   (a) State __Wisconsin__ (b) County __Vernon__
   (c) If rural _____ Give township (not postoffice) or City or Village __Genoa__
   (d) Street No. _____

MEDICAL CERTIFICATION

3. (a) Full Name __Bartholomew R. Venner__

5. (b) If veteran, name war __--__   5. (c) Social Security __--__

4. Sex __M__   5. Color or race __W__   6. (a) Single, widowed, married, divorced __M__

6. (b) Name of husband or wife __Mary N.__   6. (c) Age of husband or wife if alive __66__ years.

7. Birth date of deceased __Nov. 17, 1873__
   (Month) (Day) (Year)

8. AGE: Years __72__ | Months __4__ | Days __30__ | If less than one day — hr.— min.

9. Birthplace __Genoa, Wisconsin__
   (City, town, or county) (State or foreign country)

10. Occupation and industry or business

Father { 11. Name __John B. Venner__
         12. Birthplace __Italy__
         (City, town, or county) (State or foreign country)

Mother { 13. Maiden name __Madeline Starlokie__
         14. Birthplace __Wisconsin__
         (City, town, or county) (State or foreign country)

15. (a) Informant __Mrs. Mary N. Venner__
    (b) Address __Genoa, Wisconsin__

16. (a) __Burial__ (b) Date thereof __4/22/46__
    (Burial, cremation or other) (Mo.)(Da.)(Yr.)
    (c) Place: burial or cremation __St. Charles Ch.Cem. Genoa__

17. (a) Signature of funeral director __Howard L. Aiken__
    (b) Address __Bellwig-Morris-LaCrosse, Wis.__

18. (a) __April 18, 1946__ (b) __Wm. Kotvis,__
    Local Filing Date   Signature of City Health Officer
    (c) State Registrar's Filing Date: _____

19. Date of death: Month __April__ Day __16__ Year __1946.__

20. I hereby certify that I attended the deceased from __Apr.16__ 19__, I last saw h_____ alive on __Dead Apr. 16__ 19__ and that death occurred on the date stated above at __2 P__ M.

21. Immediate cause of death __Coronary Occulsion__   Duration _____
    Due to __Gen.Arterio sclerosis__

    Other conditions _____
    Include pregnancy within 3 months of death

    Name of operation __CERTIFIED COPY__ Date _____

    Major findings __NOT VALID__   Underline cause to which death should be charged statistically.
    __FOR IDENTITY PURPOSES__

    Autopsy Performed? Yes __ No __

    Findings: _____

22. If death was due to external causes, fill in the following:
    (a) Accident, suicide or homicide _____ (b) Date _____
    (c) Where did injury occur? _____ (City, village or township, county and state)
    Did injury occur in or about home, on farm, in industrial place, in public place? _____ While at work? _____
    (Specify type of place)
    (e) Means of injury _____ (Fall? Auto? Machinery? etc.)

23. Signature __G.G.Raleigh__ (M. D. or other)
    Address __La Crosse, Wis.__ Date signed __4-17-46.__

Certificate of Death
Mary Caroline Venner
18 September 1947

Form No. 206—12-46—50M
Copy Certificate of DEATH

WISCONSIN STATE BOARD OF HEALTH 507
Bureau of Vital Statistics Local Registrar's No. 517 — 83

Please Cooperate. Use black ink to improve a photostatic copy of this record for legal purposes.

1. PLACE OF DEATH:
   (a) County La Crosse
   (b) Township or City or Village La Crosse
   (c) Name of hospital or institution St. Francis

2. USUAL RESIDENCE OF DECEASED:
   (a) State Wisconsin (b) County Vernon
   (c) If rural _____ Give township (not postoffice)
   City or Village Genoa
   (d) Street No. Main Street

MEDICAL CERTIFICATION

3. (a) Full Name

3. (b) If veteran, Mary Caroline Venner
   name war ____ No. ____   5. (c) Social Security

4. Sex female race white 6. (a) Single, widowed, married, divorced widowed
   (b) Name of husband or wife alive Bartholomew 6. (c) Age of husband or wife if alive ____ years.

7. Birth date of deceased Feb. 20, 1880
   (Month) (Day) (Year)

8. AGE: Years 67 Months 6 Days 18 If less than one day ____ hr. ____ min.

9. Birthplace Norway, Michigan (State or foreign country)

10. Occupation and industry or business Domestic

Father: 11. Name John Nicolatti
        12. Birthplace Austria (City, town, or county) (State or foreign country)

Mother: 13. Maiden name Margaret Gaberial
        14. Birthplace Austria (City, town, or county) (State or foreign country)

15. (a) Informant Mrs. Alois Pedretti
    (b) Address Onalaska, Wis.

16. (a) burial (Burial, cremation or other) (b) Date thereof 9-23-47 (Mo.)(Da.)(Yr.)
    (c) Place: burial or cremation St. Charles Cem. Genoa, Wis.

17. (a) Signature of funeral director Howard L. Aiken
    (b) Address La Crosse, Wis.

18. (a) Sept. 20, 1947 Local Filing Date (b) A.A.Horachek Signature of City Health Officer or County Register of Death
    Deputy

19. Date of death: Month Sept. 18 Year 1947

20. I hereby certify that I attended the deceased from Sept. 3, 47 to Sept. 18-47; I last saw her alive on Sept. 18-47 and that death occurred on the date stated above at 8 p. M

21. Immediate cause of death

	Duration
Subarachnoid hemorrhage	9/17/47
Due to	
Arteriosclerosis	yrs.
Other conditions	

Include pregnancy within 3 months of death

Name of operation ____ Date

Major findings Of operation

Autopsy? No
Performed

Findings

CERTIFIED COPY
NOT VALID
FOR IDENTITY PURPOSES

Underline cause to which death should be charged statistically.

22. If death was due to external causes, fill in the following:
   (a) Accident, suicide or homicide ____ (b) Date
   (c) Where did injury occur? ____ (City, village or township, county and state)
   (d) Did injury occur in or about home, on farm, in industrial place, in public place? ____ While at work? (Specify type of place)
   (e) Means of injury ____ (Fall? Auto? Machinery? etc.)

23. Signature J.E.McLoone
    Address La Crosse, Wis. Date signed 9/19/47

Autopsy Report
Agnes Pedretti
Death 11 December 1978

Edward B. Maier, M.D.
William A. Morgan, M.D.
Kermit L. Newcomer, M.D.
David D. Norenberg, M.D.
Edwin L. Overholt, M.D.
Anthony S. Pagliara, M.D., Endocrinology and I
Francisco Perez-Guerra, M.D., Pulmonary Disea
Edward L. Perry, M.D.
Bruce A. Polander, M.D.
Robert W. Ramlow, M.D.
Martin J. Smith, M.D., Hematology
Duane W. Taebel, M.D., Gastroenterology
James W. Teeman, M.D.
John B. Weeth, M.D., Medical Oncology
Edward R. Winga, M.D., Pulmonary Disease
Wilfrido R. Yutuc, M.D.

Mr. Bernard Pedretti
Route 1, Box 374
Prairie du Chien, WI 53821

Dear Mr. Pedretti:

The initial autopsy findings on your mother reveal extensive arteriosclerosis involving the blood vessels of the heart as well as of her
brain. Similar findings were also seen in other blood vessels through-
out the body. The heart muscle was somewhat thickened consistent with
her known high blood pressure for which she had been treated in the
past.

The heart vessel abnormalities are certainly consistent and expected
findings. As stated, with sudden death occurring this almost always
has to be related to some heart abnormality. When the final results
are known, I will forward them on to you.

Again, I extend my sympathies to you and your family on your mother's
passing.

The final autopsy report on your mother is now completed. This
shows significant arteriosclerosis with marked narrowing of the
blood vessels of the heart. Similar changes were noted in the
blood vessels in her head as previously reported. The heart
muscle was thickened; this is a change seen in individuals who
have had high blood pressure for an extended period of time.
The blood vessels of the kidney revealed arteriosclerotic changes
and also on microscopic examination there were some changes noted
in the blood vessels resulting from high blood pressure.

The pancreas revealed loss of the cells which produce insulin.
This in turn results in diabetes.

If there are any questions or if any additional information can
be provided, please do not hesitate to contact me.

Sincerely,

Kermit L. Newcomer, M.D.

KLN:jh

Synopsis of *The Story of Our Stories*

The Story of Our Stories is the story of Maria Prima and Maria Therese, Peter and John, Adelaide and Stefano, Agnes and her children, and especially the individuals who peopled the Mount of San Bernardo and the Valley of Saint James the Lesser who turned the roughness of Bad Ax into the gentleness of Genoa, Wisconsin—but first and foremost it is our story, the story of you and me. Our story is written as an epic composed of twelve books, each with a supportive appendix. Each book covers a different measurement. Some cover the life of a typical family member of a specific generation, others reflect many people of a generation, another traces the entire story from beginning to now, and one looks into a future predicated by the behavior of our mothers. Each volume tells a critical part of the story, is an integral part of the whole, and plays into the unfolding of the epic. While arranged by number, each book can be read independent of the rest.

Book 1: *Time to Journey Home*—This is a travelogue about my trip back to the homeland and how I was inspired to write *The Story of Our Stories*. The appendix includes a pre-1909 ahnentafel history of the author, autobiographies of select persons who researched the family's ancestry, a manifesto calling for a new epic, and the story of rough-and-tough Bad Ax evolving into Genoa, Wisconsin—the home of a spray drift of calm. The closing essay in this book reveals the great inequality perpetrated by the Social Security Act and offers a fail-safe solution to equalize and perpetuate Social Security ad infinitum.

Book 2: *The Veneid*—This epic poem tells of a journey into our past (similar to the *Divine Comedy*) where the poet meets many of our mothers, who celebrate woman and kindness (contrasting to the *Aeneid*'s celebration of man and war). The appendix includes the Geno outline of the female linage going back to Eve, traces the ahnentafel of the mothers, provides a chronology of major events, includes an essay on the supremacy of stories, and offers selections from *The Truly Short History of Man.*

Book 3: *Begetters of Children*—This work of historical fiction shows how the branch of one family settled on San Bernardo Mountain in Lombardy, Italy; developed a village; farmed unfarmable land; avoided plagues, wars, and other human disasters; had many children; immigrated to Genoa, Wisconsin; developed the land; and populated half of America (I joke only a little here). The appendix includes an article on the role of epic literature in shaping human perspective, a history of the founding and development of the mountain town of San Bernardo accompanied by the historical evolution of a republic government in Val San Giacomo, the ahnentafel story of Stefano Pedretti, and facsimiles of vital records of San Bernardo.

Book 4: *Lost Book of Valle di Santa Maria Prima Della Morte*—This novel is based on Giovanni Vener's revelations about the life and accomplishments of his grandmother Maria Prima Della Morte (1758–1817). The appendix includes the genealogical history for Giovanni Vener (born 13 March 1829), the story of Campodolcino and Val San Giacomo, primary documents showing vital information of Giovanni's ancestors, a short work clarifying the illogicality of classism, an essay on the failure of the second amendment to protect freedom, and an article catechizing the god story.

Book 5: *L'Ultima Preghiera*—Marie Teresa Cerletti-Pedretti speaks her last prayer aloud a day or two before her death on January 29, 1853, as she realizes that her Maker has called her too early, before she can raise her family and prevent her elder sons from abandoning their heritage to the dream of a better future. The appendix tells the stories of the major churches of worship where the baptisms, marriages, and funerals of our characters took place, presents Maria Teresa's ahnentafel, explores the transitional year 1848, and includes Maria Teresa's letter to her children on the beginning of life.

Book 6: *Lettere d'Amore*—Stefano Pedretti and Adelaide Lombardi wrote a score of letters while courting each other at great distances in 1853 and 1854. The last letter is written by Adelaide forty years after she tragically lost the love of her life to a freak lumber accident. The appendix includes the ahnentafel of Adelaide Lombardi, tracing her family back to Airolo, Switzerland; the story of Airolo; primary documents of Adelaide's ancestry; photographs of our main characters' gravestones; an essay identifying the three stages of love; and observations on the immanent failure of compromise to resolve anything.

Book 7: *Diary of Giovanni Vener: An Immigrant's Journey to the Heat of America* — selections from the diary of a pioneer written while incarcerated in the Vernon County Insane Asylum at the turn of the century. John Venner spent the last days of his life confined, and his diary fluctuates between manic and depressed days. Readers glimpse inside of the head of an immigrant reliving the high points and the low points of being an innovator on the frontier. The book includes the second half of the story of Genoa and a manifesto by a great-grandchild of John calling for the end of famine, pestilence, and war—the trinity of premature death.

The appendix includes a score of facsimiles of Genoa postcards, and ancestral notations of Giovanni's wife, Mary Madeline Starlochi, supported with primary documents found during the research of Starlochi family.

Book 8: *Peter Profile* describes a transitional figure who dominates his community as the world leaves the age of horse and buggy for petrol-powered mass transportation. Peter Pedretti was the wisest man I ever met. He raised eleven children, mostly by himself as his wife died shortly after the birth of their youngest daughter. The appendix includes the story of Gofis, Austria, home of the Malins and Petlarnbrand; Tochov, Bohemia, home of Maggie's mother; photos of Peter's homes and farms; the ahnentafel of Peter's wife, Maggie Malin; an essay by Peter offering a path to making an ethical life; and selections from the multi-year Sunday-morning discussions between Peter, a progressive thinker, and his conservative brother Stephen, agreeing often on goals but separated on policy and implementation.

Book 9: *The Book of Agnes*—A novel based on one of Giovanni's granddaughters, Agnes. It is a tale of the extraordinary life of one woman's gentle manner, kindness, and fertility over forty summers and forty winters, when capitalists' greed undermined the economic stability of the world, a deranged ethnic population inspired by a maniac caused the death of fifty million people, and Soviet panic all but knocked out any remaining American sense and led to numerous wrongful wars. Walt Whitman had Agnes in mind when he eulogized the "numberless unknown heroes equal to the greatest heroes known." The appendix includes mini-biographies of Agnes's siblings and in-laws; the ahnentafel chart of Agnes' mother, Mary Caroline Nicolatti; the story of Trento and Trentino, the homeland of the Nichelati family; a letter from Agnes calling us to put X back in Christmas; and a treatise asking the ultimate question: What does it mean to be human?

Book 10: *Hoe-ers: Twelve Stories by Twelve Siblings*—The autobiographies of twelve of Agnes's fifteen children are accompanied by the imagined dairies of two others. You will often read about the same events told from different perspectives. The appendix will include the story of the forty double cousins—the grandchildren Peter & Adelaide Pedretti and Tom & Mary Venner—along with the Geno story, tracing their paternal roots back to Northern Europe, the Middle East, Africa, and ultimately to Mitochondrial Adam. The concluding essay in this book will demonstrate that our worship of work—"get a job"—is nothing more than the continuation of the entitled keeping indentured serfs at service to their avarice, complemented by a tract calling for a maximum (as opposed to minimum) wage. A special section will include the creative writings of select "hoe-ers."

Book 11: *Mick: Planter of Seeds*—Selections from the author's memoirs show a farm boy becoming a college professor and going on to become an international arts festival impresario, renovator of abandon homes, and writer of this epic. The appendix will include the ahnentafel of our author covering upwards of 480 ancestors, a photo essay telling with pictures and words the story of the immigrants who played the central role of turning this story into an epic, and select primary documents from the international theater festivals made by the author. The main essay will present the revolutionary view that life on earth is made up of trinities and not of dualities or singularities.

Book 12: *Il Lavoro di Artisti*—Book 12 presents a collection of artwork created by members of the family born into the fifth generation (the grandchildren of Agnes). Their work exemplifies that this family makes art instead of going to war to express their creative energy. The appendix will include the story of the children of Peter Pedretti and Bartholomew "Tom" Venner, including some fun facts about the families, a short thesis suggesting a radical reordering of representation in the US House of Representatives, and an essay demonstrating that the arts provide the exemplary methodology of education. The main piece is a manifesto by a great-grandchild of Giovanni Venner and Stefano Pedretti calling for the end of nation-states, monotheism, and weapons of destruction—the primary architects of war for the past three thousand years.

Note: The contents of these books are subject to change.

Other Books by Michael Pedretti
Begetters of Children
Time to Journey Home

Works in Progress
The Story of Our Stories [12 volumes]
Delighting the Senses [2 volumes]
The Truly Short History of Humanity
the dog and i: 27 poems
Little Book of Truths
Fifty Questions
The Trinity
45 by 45